MASTER
THE
MATRIX

7 ESSENTIALS
FOR
GETTING THINGS DONE
IN
COMPLEX ORGANIZATIONS

< WORKING CROSS-FUNCTIONALLY AND

MASTER
THE
MATRIX

7 ESSENTIALS
FOR
GETTING THINGS DONE
IN
COMPLEX ORGANIZATIONS

< WORKING CROSS-FUNCTIONALLY AND

BY

SUSAN ZELMANSKI FINERTY

For my Mom, Jeanine Bentley Zelmanski (1937-1998):
Not exactly what you imagined (kind of like me).

Since its introduction,
Master the Matrix has become the gold standard resource for **Fortune 500** companies, **not-for-profits**, **privately-held** companies, **universities**, and a variety of complex organizations around the **world**.

Praise for Susan Finerty's Master the Matrix

"For years the challenges of matrix management have shown up in my conversations with leaders. And for years I have been referring those leaders to one source of wisdom - Susan's "Master the Matrix". A second edition? Even better!"

STEVE KING
RETIRED EVP OF HUMAN RESOURCES AT HEWITT ASSOCIATES

"Master the Matrix is a vital resource, not just in large, complex organizations, but in everyday work life. Understanding the principles that Susan artfully and efficiently lays out are to work what gravity is to walking: once you grasp and integrate these ideas, your work effectiveness will go from crawling to running!"

BILL FLEMING
PRINCIPAL, SEGMENT RISK, LTD (LONDON, UK)

"As our world went through incredible change the last two years, it had a profound impact on workplaces. Susan's continued work on matrix management is now more insightful than ever and provides pracitcal ways to navigate and thrive in this complex and rapidly changing work environment."

ART MOLLENHAUER

"How I wish I had Master the Matrix when I started working in global firms! All too often, leaders simply acknowledge the organization is matrixed but offer no real help to those new to matrixed organizations, let alone the practical steps for not only navigating but mastering the matrix as Susan Finerty provides."

DAN GEORGE
FORMER BIG 4 SENIOR EXECUTIVE, FOUNDER
FRONT SEAT LEADERSHIP

"Susan's research and ability to translate her knowledge and insights into practical tactics have benefited thousands of business professionals across a wide range of industries."

HELEN BRAUSEN
SENIOR DIRECTOR OF CLIENT EXPERIENCE
CENTER FOR PROFESSIONAL AND EXECUTIVE DEVELOPMENT
WISCONSIN SCHOOL OF BUSINESS

"Susan's deep work provides both the art and science of cross-functional navigating to impact businesses positively. Susan's work has inspired me to create better personal and professional strategies for collaboration, communication, and developing interpersonal relationships to optimize my professional, organizational, and client success."

SHABNOOR SHAH
OPEN LEADERSHIP GLOBAL & EXECUTIVE COACH
RED HAT OPEN INNOVATIONS LABS & TRANSFORMATION SERVICES

"Master the Matrix is one of the simplest and most useful tools to make an impact and be successful. A total game changer, I wish I'd found it earlier in my career."

DEB SKARDA MSN, MBA, PCC

"In order to deliver customer and financial outcomes in today's complicated and digitally influenced business environment, leaders and employees need to solve for multifaceted challenges that cross business units and functional boundaries. Susan's book provides a practical guide for navigating complex work and organizational structures through meaningful partnerships, influencing skills, and effective communications."

RAJ PATEL
VP WORKFORCE EXPERIENCE & SR. HR BUSINESS PARTNER

"Master the Matrix has been an incredibly relevant book since it was launched. Our organization embraced it immediately. Now, more than ever, we need to be able to effectively work in a matrixed environment - and truly understand what this means. Our very success demands this. Thank you, Susan, for your continued knowledge, research, understanding and strategy for this "survival guide".

NANCY ZILIOLI EVANS

"Understanding a matrix organization is crucial in the complex world of higher education. Susan Finerty is lucid and thoughtful, and I use her advice and wisdom daily."

A. G. RUDD

Contents

2022 Foreword   i

2012 Foreword   v

Author's Note: 10 Years Later   ix

A Tale of Two Partners   1

Defining Matrix Organizations and Cross-Functional Work 4
Our Analogy: Evolving from Lanes to Intersections to Traffic Circles 5
It's Not about the Boxes 7
What Type of Matrix Role Are You in? 8
We Know It When We See It 9
The Building Blocks 10
A Quick Look at the Research 12
Caveat Emptor 14
Getting the Most out of This Book 16
Beyond the Book 17

Start with Partnerships   19

Who Should Your Partners Be? 21
The Matrix–Partner Continuum™ 23
The Four Matrix Partnership Types 24
Do You Have the Right Fit? 27
The Partnership Mindset: Don't Wait for Them 29
Be Deliberate: Partnership Investments 31
Pulling Back: When Your Partnership Overreaches 40

Get Goals Aligned   45

The Two Types of Matrix Goal Misalignments 47
Four Ground Rules for Goal Alignment 47
Align from the Start and Then Realign as You Go 49
Channeling and Cultivating Natural Misalignments 54
Preventing Human-Made Goal Misalignments 56
Resolving Human-Made Misalignments: Pick Your Battles 58
Partnership-Driven Resolution 59
Rules of Elevation 60
A Note on Goal Alignment and Rewards 61

Clarify Roles   67

Getting Things Right from the Start: Defining Roles 70
Three Simple Guidelines for Using Role Clarity Tools 72
Dealing with Boundary Breach 74
Why Boundary Breach Happens 75
When to Tackle Role Conflicts 76
Partnership-Driven Resolution for Role Conflicts 77

Last Resort: Elevate It 78
Sorting Out Solid and Dotted Line Responsibilities 79

Get Decisions Made   85
Key Differences between Decision-Making in Traditional and Matrix Roles . . . 86
Five Rules for Getting Decisions Made in a Matrix Role 87
Rule #1: Balance and Toggle Your Decision-Making Styles 88
Rule #2: Watch Your Biases 92
Rule #3: Set It Up Right 93
Rule #4: Invest in Agreement 95
Rule #5: Go the Extra Mile to Make Sure the Decision Sticks 98
What's at Risk: Decision Splintering 99
A Final Word: Winners and Losers 100

Flex Your Influence Muscle   105
Building Influence Muscle in Matrix Roles 107
Deciding to Wield Your Influence Muscle 108
Influence Ingredients: Proactive and In the Moment 110
Three Proactive Ingredients 112
Three Ingredients for Influence in the Moment 113
The Power of Patience and Perseverance 119

Communicate Without Assumptions   125
Assumptions and What They Lead To 128
Undercommunicating 129
Overcommunicating 133
Cast a Wide Net: Communicating with the Right People 135
Yours Is Not Theirs: Communicating in the Right Way 136
Assumption-Free Listening 138

Make Meetings Matter   145
It Starts with the Right Mindset 147
Six Steps to Meetings That People Actually Want to be Part of 148
The Six Steps: 149
Step 1. Attempt to Talk Yourself out of It 149
Step 2. Get Very, Very Specific on Outcomes 150
Step 3. Craft Your Agenda (Hint: It Is Not a List of Topics) 151
Step 4. Invite the Right People and Get Them Prepared 152
Step 5. Facilitate the Heck out of It 155
Step 6. Follow Up and Hold Accountable 161
When You Aren't Leading the Meeting 161

Bonus Material: What to Hire For   166

Putting It All Together   168
So You Have Finished the Book, Now What? 168

Acknowledgments   170

About the Author   172

2022 FOREWORD

In 2009, John Deere announced an ambitious effort to find the next chapter of value creation in its 172-year history. It was a monumental shift for the company, involving the collapsing of over 65 business units at the factory level into five global platforms and the consolidation of country-level management into four major geographies. Key to success in this operating model was the notion that the leaders of the five platforms and the four geographies had to have aligned goals, with thousands of employees below them also needing to coordinate and align around new roles and responsibilities.

At the time, I was the Global Marketing Manager for Large Tractors. With this announcement, I would also be the last. Change happens. My old position was eliminated, and my new role, created in the reorganization, was leading Strategic Marketing for North America with responsibility for all agricultural and turf products.

It was my first exposure to a matrix organization. For the first time, I had multiple bosses to please, each with specific—and sometimes competing—goals concerning market share, customer satisfaction, profitability and product development. My situation was replicated in hundreds of other mid-level management positions around the enterprise.

The headaches quickly followed. For starters, it was difficult to determine who had the power to make a decision. Elaborate spreadsheets were created, listing over 80 key activities, that attempted to articulate the RACI (Responsible, Accountable, Consulted, and Informed) relationships. Next was the issue of prioritization. Large meetings of stakeholders were called on a regular basis to deliberate what goals and objectives took priority. Nobody wanted to create conflict in the new organization, and ultimately this slowed everything down.

But as these challenges emerged, there were also substantial gains. Our talent shifted from parochial to global mindsets. The focus on customer needs intensified like never before. The movement away from a factory-centric to a platform-led business structure meant better decisions on manufacturing, better investments in product design, and ultimately far fewer decision-makers than before.

After two years, it was time for a health check, and a consulting group was brought in to analyze the enterprise implementation of the change. By this time, I had moved to our Intelligent Solutions Group (ISG) and was leading a group of approximately 1,000 employees around the world designing, developing and adopting technology into our agriculture equipment.

The consultants concluded the problems we were facing were not a result of the design of the operating model, but more rooted in how we activated the model. It was the interactions that mattered. The behavior among the new relationships was the key to success.

I had the opportunity to spend some time with one of the key consultants hired to perform the assessment, and I asked him point-blank where I could learn how to effectively operate in a matrix organization.

He replied, "If you really want to know how to be good in a matrix operating model, you need to talk to Susan Finerty."

I first met Susan after reading her book, *Master the Matrix: 7 Essentials for Getting Things Done in Complex Organizations*. I had ordered 50 copies to distribute among senior leaders at ISG. I spoke with Susan soon after and invited her to do a workshop with my extended leadership team. We needed to fully understand the nuances of being effective as leaders in a matrix world. We walked through the 7 essentials and how to apply them using the 4 building blocks of Mindset, Jujitsu, Zoom Out, and Triage. At a core level we began to understand that we needed to adapt to a new way of creating value if we were going to be effective.

A few years later I was in a different role, leading the sales organization for John Deere Financial in North America. A familiar terrain emerged in this new role where the finance unit had financial goals and the enterprise had equipment, market share, and profitability goals. Each of us had our areas of focus, but to be successful we had to work hard, together, to get the job done. Enter Susan Finerty and her expertise on matrix organizations. It was an easy call to have Susan come in and perform two workshops with over 70 senior leaders to learn how to apply the 7 essentials and use the 4 building blocks.

Today I think back to those workshops and how they helped our organizations mature and evolve in the right way. The matrix operating model was exactly what the company needed at that time. But without activating it and learning new behaviors in this model, we would have never been successful.

Susan Finerty, through her book, games, and workshops, helped us navigate these issues and build strength through our implementation.

I remember the lessons I learned well during that time. Eight come to mind:

- Working in a matrix takes practice and you must take action to learn it right
- Leadership behavior is critical to success and sets the tone for change
- It takes courage to lead in a matrix environment
- You will rarely have all the cards in your hand to do what you need to if you work in a complex, global organization
- When you see good matrix behavior, call it out and help others learn the right way
- When you see problems or conflicts, use matrix techniques to highlight learning opportunities
- Meetings are sacred time—observe, inspect, adjust, and constantly improve use of time
- The new normal is conflict—expect it as a normal course of getting important work done and make conflict a positive, constructive sign of a healthy organization.

It's been nearly 10 years since I first called Susan and asked for her help. Over the years I have kept in touch with Susan to learn how organizations continue to apply matrix principles. It was particularly helpful to talk to Susan through the pandemic and learn how companies were adapting. She also shares with me how her thinking has adapted as well. From our first conversation to the most recent one only last month, her commitment to helping leaders and organizations improve hasn't slowed down one bit. In fact, I believe it has accelerated with her latest research culminating in this new edition.

She has done the research to know what works, how it works, why it works, and the best way to implement it. She knows all this because she has taken the time to test her ideas so that we may all benefit from them.

I hope you get as much as I have out of Susan's advice and coaching. Whether you are brand new to the working world or a seasoned executive, her concepts will help you be more successful. If you commit to implementing Susan's ideas, not only will your business substantially increase the odds for success, but you will also grow into a more effective leader.

TONY D. THELEN
John Deere Financial
January 2022

2012 FOREWORD

During my 23-year career at Baxter International, I often encouraged our team members to "manage the intersections!" We were a global, multidivisional corporation, and there were plenty of intersections—global goals intersecting with local needs, functional initiatives intersecting with business decisions. I knew that this thing we called "the matrix" wasn't going away. I truly believed that we needed to find a way to use the matrix to optimize the entire organization, versus trying to optimize each part individually.

Not only was "the matrix" not going away, figuring out how to leverage it became our competitive advantage. Managing the often unclear and ambiguous matrix is a capability so uncommon that mastering it can be the difference between a good company and a truly outstanding one.

But mastering the matrix isn't just an organization's competitive advantage. It is your competitive advantage. That's difficult to see, and we may find ourselves complaining or wishing it away. The key is to take a big step back, get your arms around the entire organization and make it work for you. That requires you to really get to know the organization, understand the intersections and view the management of those intersections as a key part of your role. The people who do this not only succeed but, even more importantly, get a lot more satisfaction out of what they do.

What Susan does in this book is provide you with the tools to make the matrix work—from how to build partnerships that ease goal alignment, role clarity and decision-making to the key skills of influence, communication and meeting facilitation that enable you to gain traction and accomplish things in a matrix role. And getting things done is really what it's all about. At the end of the day—have you made a difference? Have you moved the organization forward? Do you feel a sense of pride and accomplishment in your work?

Susan also provides us a framework for discussing and assessing what it really means to "manage the intersections." With the tools in this book, when we run up against a barrier, we can diagnose it and work to resolve it.

Organizations are becoming more complex and so are our roles. Your tendency may be to try to avoid or ignore the matrix, simplify or narrow your scope, working only within the confines of your role or team. When you are tempted to do this, reach for this book. Mastering the matrix—not oversimplifying it, discounting it or hoping it goes away—is the key to your success...enjoy your journey.

HARRY M. JANSEN KRAEMER, JR.
Author, From Values to Action: The Four Principles of Values-Based Leadership
Professor, Northwestern University's Kellogg School of Management
Former Chairman and CEO, Baxter International

AUTHOR'S NOTE: 10 YEARS LATER

When I think about the period from 2010 to 2012, the years I wrote the first edition of *Master the Matrix*, it seems like a much simpler time. Sure, our organizations and work were complex (so much so that I felt compelled to use the word in the book title, much to the chagrin of many advisors), but the atmosphere seemed more straightforward. The air we breathed felt lighter, easier to move through.

As I sit here in February 2022, it's hard to see anything simple about the work we do or the contexts within which we do it. But as I read through the book again for the first time in a long time, I found simple, timeless pieces of advice that have worn well and even give comfort.

It still goes back to those 7 Essentials—partnerships, goals, roles, decisions, influence, communication and meetings. In this new edition, I have updated examples and terminology and added a lot of new tips and ideas, but those 7 Essentials didn't change. I didn't read through them and think, "Well, that one's not important anymore," or, "How could I have missed this one?" The framework, which has been validated and tested through the dialogue and questions of tens of thousands of readers, workshop participants, e-learning students and clients, works.

I shared these approaches with our three-generation workforce, and they tried them out, reported back and confirmed that we are on the right track. When the world went virtual and things got exponentially more ambiguous, we kept learning and sharing and watching to see if it would change the framework. The new reality added emphasis and nuance, but it didn't change the fundamentals of the model.

All this gives me a feeling of validation, but I am far from satisfied. There is still much work to be done; still only 44% of companies offer formal learning and onboarding about anything cross-functional or matrix in nature. Only 38% deliberately hire for it. We still try too hard to eliminate the inevitable ambiguity of matrix organizations through policy and process, instead of leveraging trust and coaching others to navigate it. We still think a core fundamental of cross-functional work—partnerships—is something we don't have time to build, and we still see meetings (our matrix work mechanism) as a nuisance.

One thing that has shifted is nomenclature. Increasingly, we refer less to "matrix" and more to "cross-functional" to describe our roles and organizations. I will use these terms interchangeably throughout the book.

I am often asked if there is any other way besides matrix structure and the expectation to work across the organization. There may be plenty of options, but your business would crumble from the financial burden and end up working at cross-purposes yet again if you decided to implement one of them. I'm not sure we have a choice. Our products are complex, which means our problems and decisions are complex, which means we have to work beyond our individual silos.

Where we do have a choice is to fight it (in the form of litanies of frustrations and constant attempts at workarounds) or to channel all that energy and decide to make it our competitive advantage. Because I am here to tell you, there's not a company out there that does this well top to bottom and side to side. Figure this out, and the competition won't even be visible in your rearview mirror.

*Unfortunately, no one can be
told what the Matrix is.
You have to see it for yourself.*

MORPHEUS, THE MATRIX, 1999

WELCOME TO THE MATRIX
A TALE OF TWO PARTNERS

FOR Rosa, it truly was the best of times and the worst of times. In describing the wealth of corporate resources she needed to work through to get her job done, Rosa stated bluntly, "There was one relationship in this corporate maze that really worked, one that was a complete roadblock and the rest were various shades of roadblock."

Rosa was in a matrix role, specifically what I call a Customer Hub Matrix. She was an HR person who relied on various centralized, corporate shared-service organizations to bring services and products to her internal customers. Rosa supported Manufacturing, which was not only geographically remote, but seemingly a world away from the culture at corporate headquarters. An idea that made perfect sense for 4,000 people at Corporate in suburban LA made no sense whatsoever to a plant of 600 in rural Mississippi or an R&D site in Galway. Rosa was at the crossroads of local needs and corporate goals.

She had five different corporate partners in her hub. Two of these provide a great illustration of the good and bad of matrix relationships. Gianna was Rosa's partner for delivering Employee Benefits to her internal customers. Fran was her partner for delivering HR information systems. The two partnerships could not have been more different.

Fran headed a group that was responsible for all human capital management systems. At the time, Fran and Rosa were both on a team charged with design

1

and implementation of a new cloud-based HR management system. Rosa also connected with Fran and her team on a daily basis to sort out more routine systems issues and projects. At first, things were smooth, and they had a few accomplishments, both for the corporate team and for the manufacturing plants. But as time went on and the stakes got higher, Rosa grew increasingly frustrated. "I couldn't figure out how to get them to provide services to my business in a way that meets Manufacturing's needs and expectations…they couldn't customize anything, had really long lead times, and they just didn't get it. It was like we were operating in totally different universes."

Any connected tasks were complicated by near-constant perceptions of trespassing onto each other's "turf." Decision-making provided regular controversy over who the decision maker was, what decisions they needed to make together and what decisions they needed to give the other a heads-up on. They rarely agreed on tactics, let alone bigger picture goals. It became a classic "throw it over the fence" relationship. HR would make a decision or create a solution and pass it over. When Rosa was asked for input on a decision or solution and provided it, she was met with, "We can't do it that way; we aren't going to customize for one group of employees." According to Rosa, "They had one way of doing things, and there was absolutely no flexibility on that. Their rules and requirements were black and white, rarely any flexibility."

"As more managers gain experience operating in matrix organizations, they are bound to spread this experience. We believe that in the future matrix organizations managers will speak less of the difficulties and pathologies than of its advantages and benefits."

HARVARD BUSINESS REVIEW, 1978

After several rounds of this, Rosa stopped giving input, and they stopped asking for it. Rosa did the bare basics to implement their work products and jerry-rigged things behind the scenes. The silos were built and reinforced with every interaction. The amount of energy consumed in silo building and the hours consumed in work-arounds were significant. The divide wasn't just between Rosa and Fran, but between individuals on their teams as well. The rift was ongoing and obvious.

Communication became more and more constricted as Rosa and Fran's trust unraveled. Doling out answers to only questions that were asked, sharing only what was absolutely necessary. Rosa described meetings as "one pack against another." At one point, a meeting that was supposed to include a total of five people representing both teams grew to 10+. There was standing room only, both teams congregating on their side of the room. Given the nature of the discussion in the meeting, it was an apparent attempt to overrule by outnumbering—on both sides.

After relaying this story to me, Rosa paused and said, "It's actually my big regret—that I didn't try harder or try a different way to make that relationship work. Surely there was something I could have done?"

She then proceeded to tell me about Gianna. Gianna was on the opposite end of the partnership spectrum. When Gianna joined the company, Rosa saw an opportunity for a fresh start with a person who she would need to work closely with. Gianna's predecessor was a reasonable partner, but in Gianna, Rosa saw the chance to form an even stronger collaboration.

She started by initiating a visit to Gianna at corporate headquarters. Then she took Gianna to a couple of plants so she could get a feel for the manufacturing culture and realities. Determined to make this work, Rosa included Gianna and her team in her meetings, readily and routinely shared information and brought them in on planning and decision-making. At first Gianna's reciprocation was scant, but it grew over time as Rosa persisted.

The partnership grew and sustained even through a few crises. "It was just so easy—there were none of the extra-curricular issues to deal with like there were with Fran and her team. It was smooth, even when times were rough." Rosa found herself far less frustrated by the fact that corporate couldn't always give her what she needed—she was willing to give and take, choose her battles. Even when decisions and solutions didn't meet 100% of Manufacturing's needs, Rosa and her team worked to implement them.

As I interviewed leaders for this book, I could tell the complexity of their matrix by the number of words it took to explain it.

The record?
462 words.

Rosa's relationship with Gianna spread to her team and her customers. Gianna's team enjoyed a unique place in the heart of the manufacturing team—the corporate team that really "gets it." In Rosa's words, "Once I had built the relationship, whether my expectations changed of what they could provide, or they provided better service, it just went a lot better. I could understand what they could really give me, where they had flexibility and where they didn't, and they understood the same from me and my business."

There are many reasons for the differences between these two partnerships—experiences and styles of the people involved, nature of the projects, even timing. These variables are not replicable, and while they might make an interesting read, the application is limited. But within this story also lie principles and practices that make matrix roles work. The partnerships that were formed, goals that were aligned (or misaligned), clarity of roles, communication and influence practices that were utilized apply in all sorts of matrix situations. So in answer to Rosa's question of whether she could have done things differently with Fran, the answer is yes. There are specific mindsets and approaches that can be applied to navigate these roles. Over the 10 years since the first edition of this book, these mindsets and approaches have been validated by thousands of participants in our workshops, coaching sessions and assessments.

The other thing that carries over from this story is the complexity of the backdrop. The maze of people and cross-functional teams that Rosa worked through is typical of corporations everywhere. Traditional structures and roles in which titles are descriptors of how work gets done are gone. They have been replaced by organizational mazes that are rarely self-explanatory.

Defining Matrix Organizations and Cross-Functional Work

"Matrix" organization structures first came into vogue in the 1960s as a way to organize around key projects in the burgeoning aerospace industry. Through the '70s and '80s, the commercial industry picked up on the trend with mixed success. Organizational design researchers Larson and Gobeli (1987) provide a workable definition of a traditional matrix organization:

> *"A 'mixed' organizational form in which normal hierarchy is 'overlaid' by some form of lateral authority, influence or communication...there are usually two chains of command, one along functional lines and the other along project lines."*

The original objective was to make sure that project team members were staying connected with their functional "home base" and serving as conduits between the project and the function—to make sure both stay in sync and weren't operating in isolation.

This attempt to link different parts of the organization together via structure took off, and we saw the emergence of not only more and more shared reporting relationships and teams, but also centralized functions and centers of excellence that worked across all parts of the organization. Organizations have moved away from a traditional business structure of multiple, independently operated business units and shifted to shared services, cross-functional teams and "flatter" organizations. All these efforts are aimed at doing more with less, gaining "economies of scale" and increasing agility. They all create the need to work cross-functionally.

In addition, automation, globalization, regulation and legislation have created a reality in which few tasks, projects or goals fall neatly into one person or team's bailiwick. Instead they cut across teams, functions and geographies. Problems stretch across multiple functions, as do their solutions and the processes for reaching them. To manage these tasks and solve these problems, organizations began to form around them, formally and informally—through full-on teams or individual reporting relationships. These matrix structures are intended to maximize the power of the juncture between global businesses and local resources, between technical expertise and business units and among multiple functions. Rosa, in the opening story, found herself at the dead center of a matrix between corporate shared services and her manufacturing customers.

In the first edition of this book, I expanded the definition of "matrix" to include not only dual-reporting relationships, but the matrix that is created as we reach up, down, side to side and diagonally across the organization to get things done. I did this because I found when I talked to people, that is how they were using the term. It wasn't just about having two bosses, it was about the web of resources needed and the working across required in their day-to-day priorities. In this new edition, I will use the terms "matrix" and "cross-functional" synonymously.

Our Analogy: Evolving from Lanes to Intersections to Traffic Circles

During the launch webinar for the first edition of this book, a participant asked a great question, "Susan, if matrix organizations are so complex that people need a book to try to understand how to work in them, why do organizations use them in the first place?" Whoa. Great question—I realized I had become so embedded in cross-functional matrix work that I failed to pull back and address a basic question.

Since then, I have refined my answer and built an analogy that has a bit of a cult following (to the point I am often called "That Traffic Circle Woman"). Our matrix organizations are truly like traffic circles—people from different directions (functions, businesses, locations) converging on a project, decision or issue, moving in the same direction and exiting when needed, while the flow of information and work doesn't stop.

But organizations usually don't start as traffic circles. They start as single lanes of traffic. In that single lane is everything needed to support the business—from resources to develop products and services to sales, marketing and support functions. For a while, they may be able to create a new lane each time they expand. Develop a new product—build a new lane. Expand into a new geography—build another lane.

But sooner or later, businesses realize that replicating lanes is a really expensive way to grow. And the more complex the product, the more expensive these lanes are. In addition, when your organization is built in lanes, people think in lanes. They don't look to the left or right to see how their decision will impact others; they do what is right for their lane.

Finally, when you have lanes as your operating structure, you lose agility, because your end users, clients, customers, patients, buyers, etc., have a lot of needs that don't fall neatly in your lanes. Operating in narrow lanes, you can lose the ability to anticipate and adjust to their requirements.

So, organizations realize the financial burden of lanes, the way they limit enterprise-wide thinking and agility, and they create intersections: cross-functional teams and project teams that bring together all parts of the business, centralized shared services that cut across all parts of the business, dotted and solid line reporting relationships that bring together two lanes through a single person's reporting relationship.

They create these intersections through organizational structure, and the matrix is born. Unfortunately, a lot of organizations stop there—with a new org chart. If your only effort to work cross-functionally is an org chart, then chances are all you have created is a traffic jam. All of these intersections slow everything down, you get people crying for a return to lanes at best, and at worst, you've got people ignoring the intersections and sailing happily down their own self-made fast lane.

A consumer product company client of mine did just that. Through no small effort, they created brand teams to support their products—an intersection of all parts of the organization converging on a single product line, managing it end to end. The intent was noble, the design elegant, but they were never truly able to gain the perspective, focus and speed they were looking for with this massive change in organization structure—without shifts in behaviors, all they got was gridlock and expensive work-arounds.

In order to reap the benefits (financial, enterprise-wide thinking and agility), you have to do more than create a structure, you have to change behavior. You need behavior more becoming of a traffic circle than an intersection.

When I am with teams, I will ask them, "What is key to navigating a traffic circle as a driver?" And they generally come up with a list like this:

- You don't stop, you have to yield
- Everybody has to go in the same direction
- There are fewer rules and it's more ambiguous, so you have use judgment
- You have to be more aware of your surroundings
- You have a different connection with other drivers

Guess what? Those five items just happen to be the foundation of working cross-functionally. In order to effectively navigate a matrix, all parties have to be willing to yield (what I call "jujitsu," more on that later), and everyone has to agree on direction (that's goal alignment). Matrix organizations are inherently more ambiguous than traditional organizations. Where there is ambiguity, you rely on judgment, broad awareness (I call this "zoom out"), and connection with others (what we will call partnerships).

If this book could be summarized in one word, it would be "flow." Traffic circles seek flow. Matrix practitioners seek flow, and this book, and the research that backs it, outlines specifics on what that takes.

> *Traffic circles seek flow. Matrix practitioners seek flow, and this book, and the research that backs it, outlines specifics on what that takes.*

It's Not about the Boxes

Researchers and authors have done considerable work examining the optimal dimensions of a matrix, structure and strategy alignment, how to implement a matrix structure, etc. Organizations frequently look to reshuffle the deck and consider how they can reorganize the matrix for better results. Some of the best work done on this topic is from Amy Kates and Greg Kesler in their books, *Designing the Organization* and *Networked, Scaled, and Agile.*

The architecture of matrix structures is important—like a house built on a faulty foundation, no amount of individual skill or diligence will keep an illogical, nonsensical structure standing. But the fact is, although matrix structures start as boxes on paper, they rely on people to work. Where this book picks up is what happens *after the boxes are laid out.* It's about the partnerships, the end game of these partnerships and the skills that get you there.

What this means is that not only can we not expect structure to drive behavior, we also can't blame structure for our behavior. A machine manufacturing client of mine was lamenting about all the behaviors and constraints their structure puts on them. I was quick to remind them that structures, at the most basic description, are lines and type on a piece of paper: "Those lines and boxes are not the boss of you," was my retort.

What Type of Matrix Role Are You in?

Matrix roles are set up to enable organizations to get the best of both worlds. An organization wants global oversight and local autonomy, so they set up a dotted line reporting relationship across geographies, connecting the goals of the global corporation and the local team. They want to support business units without recreating support teams all over the company, so shared service teams are created, bringing the competing priorities and goals of business units to the desks of the team members. To ensure that product design teams stay connected with the business and the customer, team members report to the project lead and to their business. To solve a problem that cuts across multiple functions with a solution that cuts across those same functions, they form cross-functional teams.

Let's get specific about your matrix role. Matrix roles can be seen above you (multiple bosses) and surrounding you (multiple, disparate stakeholders you depend on). Some of the most common matrixed roles are:

FORMAL PROJECT MATRIX

This is the most "traditional" and established form of matrix. It is defined as having a project management office structure and a functional or business reporting structure. These roles are very common for long-term projects like product development. People are generally 100% allocated to these projects/positions. The idea behind this is to establish dedicated resources that utilize structured project management, but are still held accountable to the function or business that owns the final product.

> *"I am an engineer on a product development project. On the 'official' org chart, I report to the Engineering Department Head. In reality I spend 80% of my time and get 80% of my work and direction from the project manager for a development team I am a part of—she's my 'dotted line' boss."*

CROSS-FUNCTIONAL TEAM MATRIX

These have cropped up all over organizations as a way to solve problems and keep the business moving. They are generally for specific (and often short-term) projects/issues. The idea behind this type of matrix is that more minds = better problem identification and better solutions.

> *"I am a member of an agile team building software that tracks clients from lead to deliverable impact measures."*

REPORTING RELATIONSHIP MATRIX

This is most often seen as an outgrowth of globalization. Often, globalization includes centers of expertise that maximize the knowledge of specialists and maintain local offices to maximize proximity to customers and markets. So while a person (say HR, Marketing, Finance) may report to a centralized head of their function or region, he or she may also have a solid or dotted line to a business or geography. This dual-reporting relationship is intended to ensure that the specialist doesn't operate in a vacuum, removed from those whom he/she supports.

> *"My boss is the VP of Supply Chain for Spain, but I work with the head of the business on a daily basis and also need to make sure that I am doing what the corporate Supply Chain team expects."*

CUSTOMER "HUB" MATRIX

Companies often have dedicated customer teams whose sole purpose is to work together to meet the needs of specific internal and external customers. More and more, these teams are not fully dedicated to one customer or even customer group. Instead they are a "shared service" that supports a line of products or even an entire business. Rosa in The Tale of Two Partners was in an internal customer hub, but they can be seen with external customers as well. It is left to the customer contact to orchestrate all that is needed to deliver on customer needs.

> *"I am the key customer contact for this territory. My company has six different divisions. My customers order products from all six divisions. Most of my job entails negotiating and executing contracts across these six divisions. I am all matrix—none of these people report to me."*

These four types of matrix roles may differ in how and why they are set up, but they have common challenges and require common underlying skills and practices.

We Know It When We See It

It may have been easy to identify which matrix role best describes your own. Plotting a course for success in your role is a little trickier.

In his opinion for Jacobellis v. Ohio in 1964, Supreme Court Justice Potter Stewart said of the French film, *The Lovers*, "hard-core pornography is hard to define, but I know it when I see it … and the motion picture involved in this case is not that."

Matrix management is a little like that—you've probably seen people who navigate cross-functional roles and organizations well. They persevere where others have given up and flourish where others have faded. But "You either got it, or you don't" isn't exactly helpful if you are trying to improve your matrix management abilities.

If you have ever sought coaching on how to steer your way through a matrix role, chances are you met with blank stares or vague suggestions. Like many skills, people who are masters of the matrix may not be able to explain what they do or why they do it. Even leaders who are great coaches may struggle with helping to develop this one—so don't be surprised if even your highly successful boss isn't conversant on the topic.

That's because we haven't given cross-functional work a real definition. We have models for coaching, frameworks for project management, templates for giving feedback. But cross-functional work has remained largely amorphous. The 7 Essentials that make up this book are a start to naming what it takes to achieve results in matrix roles:

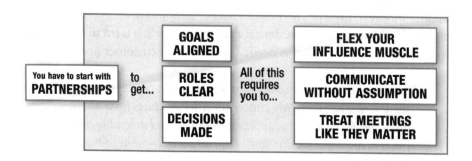

The Building Blocks

In my original research for this book, I started seeing common threads to the success stories I heard, as well as consistencies in the less-than-successful scenarios described. I call these common foundational elements Building Blocks, and they are woven throughout the book:

MINDSET   JUJITSU   ZOOM OUT   TRIAGE

You will see icons in each chapter that pull out ideas related to these elements. They serve as an "at-a-glance" view of key tips and ideas.

MINDSET

Adjust your thinking from lanes and intersections to traffic circles and you are halfway to becoming a matrix master. In *The 7 Habits of Highly Effective People*, Stephen Covey does a great job of explaining how the way you think about something affects your actions and ultimately outcomes. He calls it the See-Do-Get Model. How you approach or see things will determine what you do, which in turn leads to your outcomes. If you want different outcomes, you need to start by changing how you view your situation—your mindset.

There are four mindsets that I think are especially important and can be applied across all essentials and cross-functional contexts:

1. Anticipating is half the battle. This book is full of the realities of matrix work. Remember these realities and anticipate them in your work. When you anticipate, you navigate quickly. When you don't anticipate, you get surprised, or even worse, you start to assume some level of associated dysfunction and get caught up thinking "this shouldn't happen."
2. At the heart of everything is trust. Every challenge you face has a relational component to it; don't try to fix anything without looking at the relationship and connection issues at the core.
3. Get comfortable with ambiguity, don't seek to eliminate it. Cross-functional work is ambiguous; there is no amount of defining, outlining or spreadsheeting you can do to eliminate it. You have to build your tolerance (and mindset #1, anticipating it helps as well).
4. Be cautious of those things that feel fast. We are constantly trying to pick up speed. There are legitimate ways to do this (some listed in this book), and there are others that feel fast (like making a call without consulting others) but in the end will cost you time.

JUJITSU

You were introduced to this concept through the "yield" in the traffic circle. Jujitsu is a 2,500-year-old martial art that relies on redirecting the force of your opponent, thereby using his/her energy, not your own. Jujitsu is pertinent to matrix masters because conflict (though generally not hand-to-hand conflict!) is what matrix roles are set up to bring out. You can view this conflict as a battle and exhaust yourself fighting, or you can choose to *not* fight fire with fire. If you don't compete (for resources, decisions, control, etc.), your opponent can't win. Instead, try stepping away or disarming the conflict by giving concessions. It may seem counter intuitive and potentially counter to your organization's culture, but it is a powerful approach that leaves your reputation, values and strength intact.

ZOOM OUT

Cross-functional work requires more awareness than traditional work, just like traffic circles require different awareness than intersections. Maintaining a narrow, siloed focus on only your small segment of a project or organization will lead to failure. Matrix Masters must be able to see all the pieces of the puzzle at once to figure out whom to involve, communicate with and influence. The traditional perspective of "I focus on this and this only" will only hurt you in a matrix role. Zooming out can be difficult because when we are overwhelmed or confused, our natural human tendency is to pull back and focus on whatever is right in front of us. These blinders may offer temporary relief, but not a sustainable solution.

TRIAGE

Triage is a medical term that refers to the process of efficiently prioritizing patients based on the severity of their condition when resources are insufficient to treat them all immediately. It comes from the French verb *trier*, meaning to separate, sort, sift or select. Working cross-functionally with a zoom-out mentality, you will see a lot: discussions that need to take place, decisions that need to be made, problems that need to be solved, conflicts that need to be resolved. But seeing them isn't the same as tackling them. To avoid being completely overwhelmed, you have to triage. I have worked with a number of Emergency Room physicians for whom triage is a way of life. Although the stakes are not quite as high in a matrix role, triage is still vital. You are privy to things you wouldn't see in more traditional roles. But you can't take it all on—you have to triage.

A Quick Look at the Research

When I started examining matrix organizations in 2010, there was no research on what makes for an effective matrix practitioner. I did enough of my own research at the time to create the 7 Essentials model and identify the Building Blocks. Hundreds of workshops, discussions and coaching sessions later, these have been vetted on the front lines of some of the most complex cross-functional roles you can imagine.

But still, as I started this second edition, I wanted some quantitative data points. So, through quick surveys of clients and colleagues and mining the data from the Matrix180 tool (a multirater tool that measures your cross-functional effectiveness and identifies what's most important in your matrix role), I found some not-so-surprising information (partnerships are key), some enlightening (partners really want to know what's going on with you) and some frustrating (we are still having too many low-quality meetings).

These research nuggets will appear at the start of each chapter, but here is an at-a-glance of what rises to the top across all 7 Essentials:

What's most important? (No real surprises here.)
- Being trusted throughout the organization
- Knowing your partners' business realities and processes—not just your own
- Knowing your role in the organization
- Providing information that is easy to understand
- Having partnerships that help you and your team get things done

Where do most people fall short? (These are pretty interesting!)
- Proactively sharing your priorities and goals with partners
- Focusing on a limited number of goals
- Knowing the priorities and goals of others
- Knowing what information partners need and proactively sharing it
- Anticipating role clarity issues versus getting frustrated when people cross into your "turf"

Which essential is most challenging?
- Goal alignment

Which essential represents the biggest potential competitive advantage?
- Decision-making

I always tell people that information needs are really, really high in cross-functional organizations, and the data bears that out. And as I am sure everyone reading this feels, we are stretched and distracted by far too many goals. And (yikes!) a lot of us can get territorial. Interestingly, if we figured those items out, we would probably get pretty good at both goal alignment and decision-making.

There will be more on all of these in each chapter, but most importantly in the next chapter—Start with Partnerships—because most of what you read above circles around the reality that partnerships are really, really important when working cross-functionally.

Caveat Emptor

Although this book is focused on the people who make cross-functional roles work, clearly these roles do not exist in a vacuum. They are part of organizations and are affected by all elements of the organization.

Herein lies my dilemma: I want this book to empower you. I want you to move from "I surrender" to "Bring it on, I can do this." Too often we give up and resort to blaming the matrix for our lack of success. I want to loosen the handcuffs that we often create for ourselves. But let's be clear: *There are times when matrix roles, even when filled by a master of the skills and practices in this book, will not work. There are times when matrix roles are not set up to succeed.* One of the best matrix managers I have ever met walked away from a role because it wasn't set up to succeed. For her, the power and politics proved too much.

How do you know if your role might not be "set up to succeed"? Consider the 6 Ps (because any business book worth its salt has a good alliteration): Pay, Power and Politics, Process and Policy, and Pedigree.

PAY

Incentive systems in organizations are a powerful pull. If that pull is not lined up with your direction, it is nearly impossible to change course. For example, if your cross-functional team is incentivized to focus on everything but your project, even if you execute the suggestions in this book to the letter, you will not be able to overcome it. If your solid line boss is incentivized to drive results that conflict with those of your dotted line boss, again, you will not be able to find success easily. I have countless clients that have seen behavior shifts just through opening up compensation discussions to all matrix "bosses." Just by having the compensation system reflect the matrix reporting relationship, they were able to see changes in behavior.

POWER AND POLITICS

The first question I ask a new client as I work to get my arms around their matrix is, "Where does the power lie?" In some organizations, the culture is such that power is out of balance—for example, I have many clients where business units have the voice and functions have no say. Sometimes there are fierce struggles for power between leaders at the top. Decisions may be centralized at the top, which means nothing gets done without a title. To work, matrix organizations and roles must have some balance of power (though not necessarily 50/50), and decision-making rights must exist below the top floor. If not, your efforts in a matrix role may be beset by minefields that are difficult to anticipate and recover from, and that can reduce risk-taking and initiative to near zero. Those with organizational power also must believe in the power of cross-functional matrix work. I had a client for several years whose matrix issues seemed intractable—we kept coming back to the same problems, year after year. In a meeting with the CEO, I realized she wasn't convinced that working in a matrix was the right thing to do and was sending signals to leaders that working in this way may not have staying power. They were never able to truly change behaviors and get the benefits because their top leader was not all in on the structure and the corresponding dissemination of power.

PROCESS AND POLICY

When formal processes for sharing information, making decisions or completing tasks require multiple layers of approval, or when centralization causes a bottleneck, matrix roles can break down. Operating in matrix roles requires both individual and organizational flexibility. There are times when process or policy may not align with matrix ways of working, but even more I see layer upon layer of process and policy built in an attempt to make the organization less ambiguous. This "scaffolding" as I call it can cripple flow, and you will never be able to reap the benefits of cross-functional work when the process and policy weigh it down.

PEDIGREE

Some organizations have widely held assumptions over who can influence decisions (which is an indisputable necessity for success in matrix roles). It may be a matter of experience. I worked in an organization where if you hadn't carried the bag—been a sales rep—then you'd never influence the commercial side. If you've never worked in a plant, good luck influencing anyone on the manufacturing side. If you haven't worked in the industry, then your opinion is discounted. It may be where you "grew up," organizationally speaking—what business, function, etc. You may eventually hold influence, but it will take an extended period of time.

My advice to you is to look at these caveats and judge them honestly. No organization has perfectly aligned incentives, a complete balance of power or policies and processes in place that support what you need to get done. You can't wait for or expect perfection, but you also can't expect to drive results when organizational barriers are insurmountable.

One more thought while we are looking at things from an organizational level. Wise cross-functional organizations know not everything needs to feed into a traffic circle. They know when to create lanes. COVID vaccine development is a great example. I didn't work with Pfizer, Johnson & Johnson or Moderna at the time, but I guarantee they gave COVID vaccine development its own lane. Growth engines for the organization and even some acquisitions (at least initially) may need their own lane. Organizations have to look at structure and approach it critically to see which parts of their business would benefit from a cross-functional traffic circle and which ones need a fast pass.

Getting the Most out of This Book

It has been my pleasure (and a source of great pride) to walk into someone's office and see this book covered in Post-it notes, or when planning a session for someone to turn to a page and say, "I used this tool—let's build it into the workshop!" It is first and foremost a resource, written for practitioners—meant to be used, not simply read.

Throughout the book, we will circle back to Rosa and The Tale of Two Partnerships, but you will also see other stories and quotes from some of the thousands of leaders who have been on this journey with me. Although I have changed their names and background information (to protect the innocent and guilty), their messages are loud and clear.

For the skimmers among you, each chapter is summarized with key concepts you need to **embrace** and ideas on **where to start**. In addition, there is a final word for leaders, teams and for those of you working virtually. One of the biggest shifts from the initial publication of this book and this second edition is the work we do virtually. The pandemic, I believe, took the ripple of the remote working trend and amplified it into a tidal wave. I don't see remote work waning in importance, and there are things that are especially important to keep in mind when we are not in close proximity with our matrix.

Hundreds of tips and ideas are presented here. Some are new, some familiar, some simple reminders. Not all will be your style, and they will have to be adapted to your situation. Some you will read and think, "Yeah, I tried that—it didn't work." When you find yourself with that thought, challenge yourself on two accounts: (1) What would it hurt to try it again? (2) The last time you tried it, did you have the right mindset? As I mentioned previously, trying tips without the right mindset will limit your results.

As with any resource, the real value is your personal commitment to trying things out and taking a risk. These tips may not work the first time, or you may feel clumsy. Give yourself a break and give others a break—it may take them some time to adjust to your new behaviors.

Beyond the Book

FINERTYCONSULTING.COM

The **Finerty Consulting website**, www.finertyconsulting.com, is packed with solutions aimed at meeting the demands of complex organizations. From daily tips to monthly featured videos, there's a wealth of materials and resources including In-Person, Digital and On-Demand Learning.

180°ASSESSMENT

Are you close to Matrix Mastery? Find out with the **Matrix 180 Assessment**, a multisource feedback instrument that provides feedback on individual effectiveness in the 7 Essentials of matrix mastery!

e-LEARNING

Master the Matrix e-Learning is a great way to encourage ongoing dialogue and learning, especially for geographically dispersed organizations. Finerty Consulting provides e-Learning modules that are interactive, practical, and application based.

WORKSHOPS

Learning to Master the Matrix workshops (virtual and in person) are perfect for anyone in a matrix role. Our bias is pragmatic, application-based learning. Our participants walk out with clear next steps and behaviors to shift.

COACHING

Want help with your particular cross-functional challenges? Our pool of coaches can help you think through strategies and approaches that work in your specific context and conditions.

"Meet them halfway with love,
peace and persuasion, and expect
them to rise for the occasion."

VAN MORRISON

ESSENTIAL #1
START WITH PARTNERSHIPS

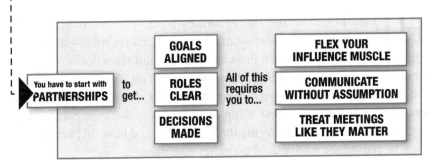

WHAT IT IS

Partnerships are integral to matrix roles, where almost no endeavor is purely independent. The most important skill a matrix practitioner possesses is his or her ability to build, maintain and repair partnerships. These partnerships facilitate goal alignment, role clarity and decision-making, which are the foundation of effective matrix management.

WHAT THE RESEARCH SAYS

What's most important:
» Being trustworthy
» Knowing the priorities and goals of others
» Demonstrating trust in others

What's most likely to trip you up:
» Proactively sharing information on your priorities and goals with others across the organization
» Knowing the priorities and goals of others across the organization

"Once I had built the relationship, whether my expectations of what they could provide changed, or they just provided better service, it just went a lot better. I could understand what they could really provide and where they had flexibility and where they didn't, and they understood the same from me and my business."

T H E last line from The Tale of Two Partners in the Introduction says it all. Matrix mastery—in all types of matrix roles—starts with partnerships like the one between Rosa and Gianna. But realistically, you don't always have the luxury of building from the ground up. You also have to get good at bringing partnerships back from the brink of disaster. This chapter is the longest and perhaps the most complex in the book, because partnerships themselves are so complex. Mastering the "who, what and how" of partnerships is critical to getting the most out of the other essentials.

In a matrix role, you are one puzzle piece that fits in with multiple other pieces that you can't always see or understand. Tasks that fall entirely under your control are rare. You are always pulling in others' expertise, approval, arms and legs for implementation. You are absolutely dependent on others to accomplish your goals. As I told a team within a large government agency (and 80/20 military to civilian in profile), in order to work cross-functionally, you have to trade power for partnerships.

Partnerships are the grease that makes this interdependence run smoothly. Partnerships allow work to flow unencumbered by suspicion, politics and micro-management. Partnerships actually take work out of the system. Think of all the extra steps you take in checking, following up and verifying when a partnership is lacking. Without strong partnerships, aligning goals takes much longer, roles need to be unrealistically defined and clarified, influence is nearly impossible and decision-making grinds to a halt. We try to make up for deficient partnerships with contracts, covenants, governance, process and policy only to have innovation and speed crushed under the weight of bureaucracy.

Partners take you at face value, even in ambiguous or ill-defined situations. They assume your best intent immediately and are ready to listen and be influenced. They are less stringent with paying back a favor in kind. Their trust can facilitate trust and influence with others, so your impact grows exponentially.

Matrix roles are set up to create conflict—which can fly in the face of partnerships. They bring together a variety of expertise and goals in the hope of finding a solution that provides the best of both worlds. Dotted lines call loyalty into question. Teams and hubs bring together many differences—goals, bosses, geographies. This inherent conflict creates tension that makes building and sustaining partnerships difficult.

Matrix roles force you to be acutely aware of whom your partners need to be and deliberate in your approach to building relationships with them. This is exactly what Rosa did when she reached out to Gianna. She knew Gianna was a key partner and took deliberate steps—visits, involvement in team meetings—to build the partnership.

The partnerships you must build in a matrix role may not be convenient or comfortable. Talking about good relationships in a negotiating setting, Fisher and Brown wrote in their classic work, *Getting Together: Building Relationships as We Negotiate* (1989): "While it is easier to build a good road across a prairie than through mountains, a good road through mountains may be more valuable than one across a prairie."

Like a road through a mountain, matrix partnerships can be difficult to forge, but the effort pays off if the destination is *mutual benefit*. Without mutual benefit, the attempt to partner can be seen as trying to create pawns or build a network on your way up the corporate ladder. The partnerships we will talk about in this chapter are sustainable, long-term, mutually beneficial partnerships that are built in an earnest way. These partnerships also need to stand up to circumstance.

A coaching client of mine did a great job with partnerships...most of the time. Here is a direct quote from one of my feedback summaries for him: "When 'in a good place,' when business is good, he is good at connecting with people. He is charismatic, intelligent and engaging. When frustrated, pressured or stressed he tends to retreat. This retreat can look like not listening, isolating, inflexibility and operating inside his head." Whether it's a person making it difficult to partner with, or circumstances making partnership challenging, the partnership still needs to happen.

In today's multitasking, geographically dispersed workforce, most partnerships don't just happen. Even when they do, we tend to be too narrow in our field of partners. Herein lies our starting point: Who should your partners be?

Who Should Your Partners Be?

"So, Gary, what's the biggest difference between your previous role and this one?" I asked, more as an introductory conversation starter than a formal question to my new client. "There are a hell of a lot more people to piss off in this role." At that point Gary was off and running. He had been in his first matrix role one year and had spent the better part of that year stepping on minefields and chasing rabbits down holes. Gary came from an academic background and was feeling the difference between the two cultures.

His relationship requirements had gone from fairly simple, one-dimensional connections with his department head and other professors to a three-dimensional matrix of potential partners. As with all matrix roles, an endless number of people had to, or wanted to, give input into what he was doing. Gary resented this and reacted by trying to build boundaries. According to Gary, "Why do I need to consult with people in procurement who know nothing about my area of expertise? They are just slowing me down." Not only did that piss people off (his words, not mine), it was leading him to make decisions and develop work products that missed the mark. In other words, the "mind your own business" approach was failing miserably.

Cross-functional roles require you to look outside of your team, your lane and your immediate geographic area to identify whom you need to work with and through. It is usually well outside the traditional "us." In Gary's case, he defined "us" as the people who shared his expertise; anyone else was "them" and wasn't allowed in.

> Matrix roles require you to look outside of your team, your silo and your immediate geographic area to identify whom you need to work with and through. **ZOOM OUT**

But Gary didn't stop there. He also lamented about the "junior" Marketing folks who were asking him questions and with whom he was supposed to consult. Frustrated by people below him hounding him, he shut them out. He didn't realize that matrix roles are level neutralizers. You will find yourself interacting and partnering with people at all levels of the organization—up, down, sideways, diagonal. The projects and issues matrix masters find themselves involved in almost always include multiple levels and functions.

So, the lesson of this story—don't be Gary. Strike the right balance between being too limiting in the parameters of whom you work to partner with (and thereby leaving critical people out) and casting too wide of a net (including, to the extreme, making such partnerships superficial and meaningless).

Start by looking at how your role is structured. Every job is divided up differently—yours may be categorized by project, customer or area of responsibility. Then ask yourself about the different people who are involved:

Hand-offs	Who do you work hand in hand with?
	Who do you hand things off to?
	Who hands things off to you?
Who has...	Power to veto your decisions or implementation of decisions?
	Knowledge, experience or expertise to tap into?
	Opinion leadership that can sway others you need to influence?
	Authority over resources needed to make or implement decisions?
Who do you need to...	Demonstrate support (in word and deed)?
	Convince or permit others to support?
	Complete a task?

This list is a snapshot—your list of partners isn't static. It changes by project, as people move in and out of a team or organization, as project scopes shrink or expand and as decisions are made. This exercise is not one that you complete and put on the shelf. Good matrix managers are constantly asking themselves who they should be partnering closely with. You don't need to be attached at the hip with each of these partners—there are gradations of partnerships to consider.

The Matrix–Partner Continuum™

Partnerships can take many different forms in a matrix ranging from simple hand-offs of information or work products to close integration of tasks and goals. The Partnership Continuum is an analytical look at partnerships and a way to triage the most important partnership you have.

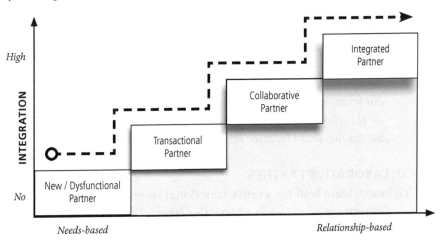

23

The vertical axis here is the degree to which partners integrate or organize their work around each other—to what extent they align goals, make decisions and plan based on the other's business. One global project leader defined the highest level of partnering as "when you are willing to change the way you do business or change your goals or your direction based on input and expertise from another person."

The Needs-to-Relationship axis is based on the degree to which the partnership is grounded solely in the business need or extended or enhanced based on the relationship. It is assumed any partnership in a matrix includes a business need (otherwise these relationships are at-will friendships), but movement through this continuum is dependent on extending beyond "I work with you because I need you" to "I work with you because you make me better at what I do."

The type of partnership is based on increasing investments (and return on those investments) in trust, communication and constructive conflict. The first two are obvious—increased trust and communication lead to more relationship-based, Integrated Partnerships. The third is less obvious because we assume that decreasing conflict is good. As partnerships evolve and integrate, more opportunities for conflict arise. However, if the partnership is strong, the ability to manage and leverage conflict also grows.

The Four Matrix Partnership Types

The four types of matrix partnerships—Integrated, Transactional, Collaborative and Dysfunctional—can be seen in any type of matrix role. Here's how I might label the partners of José, a finance director for a business unit in an insurance company:

1. INTEGRATED PARTNER
Phil, VP of Finance (solid line boss):
> "I am quickly becoming the resident expert on the operations of my business, and he depends on that. I depend on him to look out for my career. I am his go-to person on a lot of things, and I don't hesitate to go to him for counsel on anything. He's gone to bat for me, and I have for him."

2. COLLABORATIVE PARTNER
Vivianne, team lead for a cross-functional team José is on:
> "We have worked together to get this team off the ground—she knows the product, and I bring the financial expertise."

3. TRANSACTIONAL PARTNER
Maureen, General Manager (dotted line boss):
> *"Relationship is fine, I go to her for approvals and reviews as I need to."*

4. DYSFUNCTIONAL PARTNER
Leena, boss of two team members on José's project team:
> *"This one is rough, I feel like I am competing with her for the time and attention of the team members. I say one thing, she says another, and the team is caught in the middle."*

There are two important realities about these partnerships. (1) All types (with the exception of New/Dysfunctional Partnerships) are perfectly acceptable as long as they fit with the business need. (2) When partnerships evolve, they generally do so in baby steps, each level a test to see return on investments in trust, communication and constructive conflict.

INTEGRATED PARTNERS
At the far end of the continuum are Integrated Partners. Your planning, decisions and problem solving involve them. You share advice and counsel. Goals are integrated/calibrated, and communication between partners is integrated into everyday processes. At this level, the partnership may even transcend individuals and be evident at multiple levels in their organizations. You consult and confer on issues that go beyond the obvious connection and business need.

Rosa and Gianna met both key requirements of the Integrated Partner—their planning and execution were harmonized, and they advocated for each other and their teams. They involved and included each other in decision-making on a regular basis. Rosa became an ambassador of sorts for Gianna's team to the manufacturing locations. Gianna added voice to the manufacturing perspective back at headquarters.

COLLABORATIVE PARTNERS
Less discrete tasks and closer coordination are the hallmarks of Collaborative Partners. Hand-offs are supplemented with regular communication to confer and debrief. Not only are there many hand-offs, but some tasks are completed hand in hand.

Collaborative Partners focus less on winning individual arguments (and therefore will give in) and more on the big picture wins at the enterprise level.

JUJITSU

Huang and Connie are a great example. They brought together two different areas of expertise—IT and nursing, respectively—on a medical informatics project for a hospital. They were able to bring the needs of both of their functions to the table and sort out what was best for the hospital and ultimately the patients. As Huang put it, "We were able to give and take. I didn't always win and neither did Connie, but keeping our eye on the prize, we got it done."

Success in these partnerships is reliant on contribution—each partner contributes not only to the work product but to each other's success. Communication surrounds the process—joint planning on the front-end, a continual exchange of information throughout and debriefs at the end of tasks, events or projects. Conflicts are almost always creative in nature (versus personal), because they are built on the foundation of reliability and trust in the partnership that precedes it. These conflicts are nonthreatening and seen as a natural and constructive part of the process.

TRANSACTIONAL PARTNERS

The Transactional Partnership is the classic provider/consumer relationship. The focus is on hand-offs and exchanges. The tasks that connect Transactional Partners are likely process based, routine and perhaps even repetitive.

Transactional Partnerships can be seen in all four types of matrix roles. One of the more natural fits is the reporting relationship matrix role. Dotted line bosses are often Transactional Partners because of separation by geography or area of expertise. A lead for a small business unit within a technology company I worked with is a great example. "Because of the importance of my business to the organization's long-term strategy, I had a dotted line reporting relationship with the head of Global Strategy. Our connection was strictly on our quarterly numbers; for everything else, I turned to the president of our business." In this example, like all Transactional Partners, the tasks are discrete and involve some exchange of information or work product.

The keys to success in these partnerships are reliability and consistency (which build trust), well-informed partners and addressing conflicts as they arise in a constructive manner. These practices ensure smooth exchanges. A strong Transactional Partnership is a well-oiled machine.

NEW / DYSFUNCTIONAL PARTNERS

New/Dysfunctional Partnerships occur where there is need but no integration. The matrix has brought people or teams together, but they remain separate in terms of their relationship—either because the partnership is too new or because they have fallen into a pattern of competing, comparing or judging the other. Take for example a cross-functional team I worked with several years ago. They were responsible for the design and implementation of a large sales meeting every year. They were trying to figure out how to improve, not their outcome (in their words, "the work product was great") but their process ("it was really painful getting there").

The leads for Sales Training and Meeting Planning were key players in the planning process. When I talked to each of them, they were clearly nowhere near integration. Despite working side by side for months leading up to the meeting, they were competing like they were on two different sides on an imaginary battlefield. Second-guessing, blaming and keeping score formed the basis of their relationship. When I asked them individually about "how things went" with the planning of the sales meeting, I could hardly get either of them to talk about anything besides each other.

These two people were critical to the success of the annual meeting, but their dysfunction was making the planning process unbearable to everyone around them. That's the danger of dysfunctional relationships—they are palpable and contagious.

The hallmark of Dysfunctional Partnerships is lack of trust—which strains communication and turns conflict into competition. The team in this example was lucky that their work product hadn't been affected—yet. They were wise enough to see that despite current success, the level of partnership wasn't sustainable and would eventually start impacting outcomes.

"People who feel they are pawns tend to be passive and useless... Slaves are the most inefficient form of labor ever devised by man. If a leader wants to have far-reaching influence, he must make his followers feel powerful and able to accomplish things on their own."

DAVID MCCLELLAND

Do You Have the Right Fit?

The three functional partnerships can be a pass-through or a destination. A relationship may start off as Transactional but move to Collaborative or Integrated based on business need, time invested and personal connection. Transactional and Collaborative Partnerships are also fine terminal points, because not all partnerships need to evolve to the Integrated level.

The three functional partnership types are also cumulative—not distinct from each other. Any Collaborative Partnership has needs to be met and transactions to conduct. An Integrated Partnership does, too, and also requires collaboration. The key is to ensure that the nature of the partnership fits the requirements of the business and that both partners agree as to the desired level of partnership.

One team I consulted with was set up as a "committee," that was even in their name, Contract Review Committee. Sitting in on their meetings, it was obvious to me that relationships between the leader and members and among the members were very transactional, partly because they were also a transient team—their membership was constantly changing. They didn't interact much outside their weekly meetings, and their understanding of each other's role and business was very narrow. The goals of the team dictated a closer connection. Because their interaction and knowledge was limited, their meetings were long, with too much explaining, re-explaining and backtracking. Without greater integration, they were struggling in terms of effectiveness and efficiency.

In addition to supporting the business need, partners must be in agreement as to the level of partnership they need. When I explained this to Anya, a U.S. marketing manager working for a Canadian company, she started to laugh. "This explains a lot," she said. "My dotted line boss in Toronto wants to be really involved, asks a lot of questions. It drives me crazy, because I see him as a Transactional Partner. I go to him on a handful of specific items, and I think he thinks we should be more collaborative, he wants to be involved in much more. We are both assuming the reporting relationship is set up for different reasons."

Let's put one of your partnerships to the "fit test." Think about a partnership you currently have, and specifically about the nature of the work you do in conjunction with the partner. Take this quick assessment:

Put an ✗ on where you are currently.

Put a ✔ where you think the situation (business need, project, etc.) requires you to be.

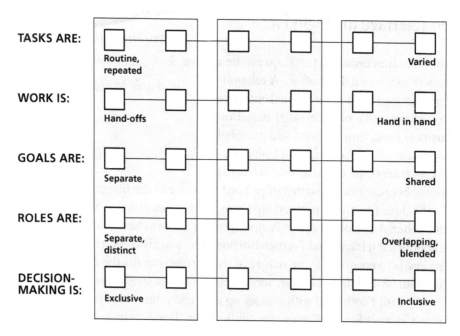

TASKS ARE: Routine, repeated		Varied
WORK IS: Hand-offs		Hand in hand
GOALS ARE: Separate		Shared
ROLES ARE: Separate, distinct		Overlapping, blended
DECISION-MAKING IS: Exclusive		Inclusive

If the majority of the ✓ marks indicating your current needs are in the left column, the situation calls for a Transactional Partnership, the middle a Collaborative Partnership and in the right column an Integrated Partnership.

Now take a look at your ✗s. Are they aligned with the needs? If they are, your partnership is well placed. If they aren't, your partnership needs a fit adjustment—you may be under- or over-investing in a partnership that should ideally be shifted more toward the right (toward Integration) or left (toward Transaction). We will talk about making these shifts in the next section.

The Partnership Mindset: Don't Wait for Them

Steve, a former COO, CFO and now C-level consultant, provides a great illustration of the shifts you need to make to your own point of view before attempting any shifts with a partner:

> "When I was the division CFO, I got along great with the CEO—Jack, my direct boss. He and I worked wonderfully together. I did not like, nor did I get along with, the corporate CFO, my dotted line guy—his name was Paulo. I don't think he liked me, either, and I just tried to avoid him at all costs. At the goal-setting time one year, the CEO said to me, "Steve, in addition to your accountabilities this year, you are going to be evaluated on your ability to create a relationship with Paulo." I said, "Jack, that's the worst thing you can ask me to do. I don't like the guy." Jack knew I didn't like the guy, and he said, "Steve, this isn't about trying to create a relationship. This is about absolutely, without question, doing it. You're going to be evaluated on this the rest of the year." So, that was a direct order and I did it. I didn't like it. It was difficult at first. But I kept at it, even when Paulo didn't reciprocate. I ended up creating a great relationship with him. The net result of that not only was tremendous success for Paulo, for me, for the CEO, but also tremendous sales and earnings breakthroughs. And a lot of it came from that relationship that I created with him. In a matrix role, you have to create relationships even when you don't want to."

Due in large part to Jack's request, Steve didn't predicate his partnering mindset or behavior on Paulo's commitment, values or behavior. In other words, he didn't wait for Paulo to change or to initiate improvements. Too often I hear people say that their colleague isn't partnering, so they themselves are unable to partner or feel it would be a waste of time to attempt to partner. This is the biggest mistake you can make. The partnership mindset is: **Don't wait for them.**

Steve demonstrated the "Don't wait for them" rule beautifully. He initiated the relationship improvement process and didn't predicate his behavior on Paulo's.

Sound impossible? Pollyanna-ish? It did to me, too, at first. A number of books helped me wrap my mind around the idea. It started with an inspirational little book called *The 100/0 Principle* by Al Ritter. The 100 piece of this equation is your behavior; the 0 is what you expect in return. Two books on conflict and negotiations, *The Triangle of Truth* by Lisa Earle McLeod and *Getting Together: Building Relationships as We Negotiate*, by Roger Fisher and Scott Brown of The Harvard Negotiation Project, apply similar models—what Fisher and Brown call being "unconditionally constructive"—to practical applications from parenting to foreign affairs. Anything that applies to nuclear proliferation—which has consequences much more far reaching than whether or not Santo supports Susie's initiative or Barb and Bob resolve conflicting priorities—surely must have some applications in the work environment.

Still doubting? Let's take a look at your choices if you are in a Dysfunctional Partnership. One of those choices is likely not whether to partner with this person or not. The matrix has brought you together for a business purpose; walking away is probably not in the cards. Your choice lies in where you elect to invest your energy:

> To build a strong partnership you invest your energy into constructive actions in line with your values, not fighting fire with fire.
>
> **JUJITSU**

Choice:	Energy spent on:
Live with it	Dealing with frustration, extra work required
Fight fire with fire	Strategizing your next move and theirs, executing your combat tactics
Don't wait for them, just change	Constructive actions that are in line with your values

It's a little like buying a home versus renting one—you either give the money away or you invest it. Either way money is spent. In partnerships, *energy* is your currency. You can choose to throw that energy into a black hole (to feed frustration, extra work, strategizing and politicking) or you can invest it in constructive behaviors that are aligned with your values and provide a role model to everyone around you, from your colleagues to your kids. It is your choice.

Before you can make any changes, you have to *change your mindset.* Especially with a Dysfunctional Partnership, you will need to change your mind about your partner. Even in a new partnership, you may need to shed your history from their predecessor or other partnerships you have had.

The first thing you must do is change your mind about your partner.

MINDSET

In the previous story, Steve's boss nudged him into changing his mind about his dysfunctional partner. We don't always have such a force to shift our thinking. Most of the time you will have to dig deep and think differently about the person on your own. If you can't do this, you will not be able to move the partnership. You have to clear your "cache" with this person, which most likely includes all sorts of behaviors, decisions and interactions that have chipped away at trust. You have to replace this history with a simple but powerful thought: "This person is worthy of a partnership." If you have to say it to yourself 500 times a day, it is worth it. Without changing your mind, your actions will be disingenuous and miss the mark. As I stated in the introduction, *trying any of the "how-tos" that form the Essentials before adopting the right mindset will make your efforts disingenuous and limit your outcomes.*

Be Deliberate: Partnership Investments

Partnerships at work are vastly different from the other relationships we form in our lives. Traditional relationships—the relationships we are used to building—are dependent on three things: proximity, chemistry and time. I refer to this as a three-legged stool.

At work, often all three legs of that stool are missing. Consider the first foundation of relationships: proximity. Most relationships we build are with people we are physically near: neighbors; classmates; members of the same team or club. They are people we "run into." In our remote work, geographically diverse and technologically separated world, we just don't "run into" people anymore. The people we need to partner with are often in a different building, on a different campus, in another state or on another continent.

The second element of most relationships is personal chemistry. We build relationships with people we like and who are like us. I have a client that I refer to as "the womb." Their mission is incredibly noble, and they are made up of people who like each other. I know that sounds great, but it trips them up. Getting them to change their mindset of "partnership = I like you" has been a challenge. Liking someone is not enough in a business partnership, and not liking someone is not a reason to step away from the partnership. It's about the work, not the chemistry. Again, at work, this is often missing—we work with all sorts of people with whom we may have nothing in common and with whom we don't connect. Sometimes we think that is a reason not to build a partnership. Nothing is further from the truth. The work brings us together with this person, not chemistry, and expecting this can lead us to miss key partnerships that can bring teams together, get a project back on track or move an initiative forward.

The final leg of the stool is time. Many of our most significant relationships are built over long periods of time—my best friend since first grade, your fraternity brother, a room parent you met 17 years ago when your kids were in grade school. But in our organizations, we don't have the gift of time. We can't always build trust over time. Instead of taking time to earn trust, we have to jump in and assume trust.

The lesson in all of this is that: work partnerships have to be approached deliberately and purposefully. They take effort. They do not grow organically; you must make deliberate effort. I define this effort as "investments," and I will outline several:

1. Trust them
2. Be trustworthy
3. Set/reset communication
4. Clean up conflicts
5. Follow the Help-Me-Help-You Rules
6. Advocate
7. Include

INVESTMENT #1: TRUST THEM

The mindset of "don't wait for them" comes through loud and clear in terms of this first behavior. You can't wait for the other person to trust you. To build trust, you must trust. Trust begets trust. Lack of trust

You can't wait for the other person to trust you. To build trust, you must trust.

MINDSET

creates more work for yourself (reviewing, controlling, attending to the extreme) and more work for them (covering, justifying, explaining), which only gets you further from trusting.

But think about what trust does—real, resilient trust is hard to defend against. Have you ever *not* trusted someone who unconditionally and genuinely trusted you? Said another way, have you ever trusted someone completely and genuinely when they didn't trust you?

Even if it's little things, you will have to start trusting them on something. Without this investment, risky as it may be, the partnership will go nowhere.

Here's what demonstrating "I trust you" looks like:

I don't trust you	I trust you
"I can't be at the meeting, we need to reschedule."	"Go on without me, I don't need to be there."
"I need to see that one more time before I am OK with it."	"I don't need to see it again, go ahead and send it out."
Cc-ing your boss or their boss	Just sending it straight out to them
Holding information until asked	Spontaneously and proactively sharing information
Needing to see it has been done	Assuming it has been done, even when you aren't there to witness it

Many of my clients are global organizations, and practitioners in these organizations will ask about cultural differences. Trust is one place where there are different starting points based on culture (the other is the degree to which conflict is addressed and how). These starting points are steeped in geographical and ethnic culture. For some interesting data on trust in different parts of the world, check out OurWorldInData.org and search "trust"—you will see different types of trust and how countries differ.

INVESTMENT #2: BE TRUSTWORTHY

Trust is a two-way street. You have to trust them, as well as earn a basic level of trustworthiness, to move out of a Dysfunctional Partnership or initiate a new partnership. When I asked Steve about where he started with Paulo, he said he just started with the bare bone basics. "I made sure I was reliable and consistent, and when I wasn't, I acknowledged it."

Reliability and consistency in a partnership means simple things like responding to questions, being on time, delivering the work product you said you would and making decisions that are in line with what you have said and done previously. And

If you waver on your commitments, be transparent about it or you risk digging yourself deeper into a difficult trust rebuilding situation.

JUJITSU

when you fail to be reliable and consistent, or really, make any type of misstep, acknowledge it. The only thing worse than making a mistake is failing to acknowledge it. People will think that you either didn't see the incongruity or assumed they wouldn't notice. If you waver on your commitments, be transparent about it or you risk digging yourself deeper into a difficult trust rebuilding situation.

INVESTMENT #3: SET/RESET COMMUNICATION

Essential #6 covers what assumptions to avoid in this process, but for now let's just talk about initial and recovery steps as applied to communication. Start with the basics. All you need to focus on here (like reliability and consistency in resetting trust) is informing—make sure they get the information they need.

To set/reset communication:

1. **Acknowledge:** Recognize your communication may have been lacking in the past and what issues that may have caused (in the case of an existing relationship).

2. **Ask:** Ask your partners what they need to know and how they want to find out. Then continue asking whether your communication is working for them.

3. **Plan:** Agree on a communication plan that outlines what, when and how.

4. **Get into a rhythm:** Cadence in communication is important. A consistent rhythm of communication (like weekly emails with a consistent, easy-to-read format or monthly discussions with a set agenda) drives comfort and trust.

5. **Careful of the "out of sight out of mind" trap:** Your matrix is likely to be physically scattered. Don't rely on the "who you see" method of remembering what and who you need to communicate with. Those who you don't run into are more easily overlooked.

Jennifer, a sales support manager, told me about some seemingly innocuous check-in meetings that got things back on track with the sales managers she worked with in the field:

> *"I sensed things were slipping, and so I instituted monthly check-ins with them. They insisted they were too busy, but I made sure I kept pushing and asked a lot of questions about what would*

be helpful for both of us. We went over progress, where we were on different initiatives and what was on the horizon. We brainstormed solutions to issues we had—I almost always walked out with a better way to work with them. It kept us informed, focused and on track in terms of our shared goals and who was doing what. We were all much more ready to be proactive because we were on top of things. After about four cycles, I felt things start to shift. We regained our confidence in each other and even comfort—it just made it easier to get things done."

Jennifer hit on many of the five set/reset behaviors. She also persisted and focused on making the check-ins meaningful not just for her but for her partners as well.

What she didn't do was wait for them to admit that they had been lousy communicators too or to ask her what communication she needed. She just focused on informing and kept doing it. She didn't waste energy identifying their shortfalls, only channeled energy into doing the right thing on her end.

INVESTMENT #4: CLEAN UP CONFLICT

If you are in a Dysfunctional Partnership, most likely you have been stockpiling. When you stockpile, you don't address a conflict, you store it. Sometimes you sweep conflicts under a rug; other times you stockpile and then dump them on your partner when you have reached a breaking point. Or maybe you are stockpiling and spreading—telling everyone but the person you have the conflict with.

Rosa was definitely stockpiling with Fran. Years later, when retelling the Tale of Two Partners to me, she vividly remembered the conflicts, the confrontations and even specific contentious conversations. At the time she thought it was the right thing to do—at first because she didn't want to rock the boat, later because she had given up hope of fixing things.

Stockpiling is a partnership killer. Even if you are not dumping or spreading the word, you can't hide stockpiling. You may think that what you are holding on to doesn't come out in how/what you communicate, how you make decisions or how you behave in general, but it does.

To reset a Dysfunctional Partnership, you have to clear the slate—either by truly letting go and forgiving or by clearing the air.

Decide what to let go or tackle based on present impact and frequency of the behavior.

TRIAGE

What do you let go and forgive? The things that have low impact—*today*. It may have been a big deal six months ago, but if it is not consequential now, let it go. Also let go of things that happened once, but aren't indicative of the partnership. You don't have to overtly forgive your partner, but mentally delete it. No longer spend any time thinking about it or talking about it. Truly let go.

Tackle those things that have high impact today—whether they happened once or a hundred times. If it impacts current results or trust in the relationship, you need to bring it up in a way that builds the partnership.

Two books that I recommend often when it comes to tricky matrix conversations are *Crucial Conversations* and *Crucial Confrontations* by Patterson, et al. (2002, 2005). These two books offer some of the most practical, realistic advice on difficult dialogue. The approach they prescribe is especially relevant to matrix relationships because of the focus, not just on resolving the conflict, but actually strengthening the relationship as a result.

The mindset for this is clearing your lens. You are putting a past issue on the table with a partner in an attempt to clear your lens, not to push them to take accountability. In fact, by focusing less on their accountability, you actually stand a better chance of getting them to take accountability—a little jujitsu in action!

> "Trust is like the air we breathe. When it's present, nobody really notices. But when it's absent, everybody notices."
>
> WARREN BUFFETT

Let's take a simple example. My client Sasha came to me recently frustrated with a partner (Miles) whose team had completely missed a critical deadline. To make matters worse, Sasha was blindsided by this fact in front of all his project sponsors. He was stockpiling this event, and as a result it was growing bigger and bigger in his mind and increasingly impacting how he viewed Miles.

I coached him through something I call "7 Minutes of Pain." That's about how long it takes just to put something on the table so you can let it go. And you can do just about anything for seven minutes.

Here's the formula I use:

Set the expectation:

> "Hi Miles, I need to talk to you about something; it's not going to be easy, and I probably won't be good at it."

This lets Miles know that he's not here to talk about the weather, and it loosens Sasha up to stumble over words or appear less than eloquent. (I personally love this approach. I think we avoid this kind of conversation because we think we have to be perfect at it—we aren't; no one is).

Simply state what you need to clear:

> *"I can't get the missed deadline from last month out of my head, and I am hoping that by just saying this out loud to you, I'll be able to let it go and move on."*

This is all about Sasha; stating it this way keeps everyone off the defensive.

Start fresh:

> *"Can we talk about how to make sure this doesn't happen again—it was brutal for my team, and I know it was for your team as well."*

Future-focused, no past to defend or explain or place blame for, simply look forward to ensure next time it works.

New partnerships don't come with a bag full of issues to resolve, but discussing potential conflicts and how to deal with them up front might make sense. It is amazing how a brief comment like, "Along the way we will probably disagree on how to manage corporate resources" makes addressing the conflict easy, safe and objective when it actually occurs. The conflict shifts from being a big deal, something that you didn't see coming or that was initiated by one partner, to something you knew would come up and you are ready to move through swiftly.

As mentioned earlier, conflict—what you bring up, if you bring it up and when you bring it up—is very driven by geographic culture. BigThink.com has an interesting "map" that plots countries on an axis from "confrontational" to "avoids confrontation" and an axis from "emotionally expressive" to "emotionally nonexpressive." This is a great framework for thinking of this issue from a cultural perspective, but I urge you to do your own "field work." If you are working globally, observe, ask questions and get really curious about the people and the cultures you are interacting with. Your direct experience and the experience of those in your matrix are the best guides.

INVESTMENT #5: THE HELP-ME-HELP-YOU RULES

There is a classic line from the movie *Jerry Maguire* that describes another investment. Jerry Maguire implores his new client to "help me help you." Good matrix partners are good customers and providers who tend to abide by a few general rules that promote good working relationships. Melissa, an account rep in a customer hub matrix, shared this story:

> *"I had a proposal that needed to get out to a client and went to the person that drafts these for me. When I walked up, I could tell she was rushed. After talking to her I found out that she was indeed working toward an important, impending deadline. She told me that she had three proposals to get out that day. I knew mine could wait 24 hours so I didn't cry wolf and tell her mine was just as urgent. I said, "Well, you know what, mine can wait until tomorrow, why don't you take care of those three and then let's talk tomorrow." It was the right thing to do, but it also told her that I don't call everything urgent—and when I do, it's for real."*

Melissa's example is a great one for several of the Help-Me-Help-You Rules. Here are the rules and what they look like from a provider and customer perspective:

The Help-Me-Help-You Rules	Provider Perspective	Customer Perspective
Don't cry wolf, ever	Don't overstate the degree of difficulty of filling a request	Don't overstate the urgency or importance of your request
Know their business	Know their business and anticipate their needs	Know and respect their processes and deadlines and make sure your request reflects this understanding. Do not expect them to make exceptions to their rules and processes, especially if your poor planning created the situation.
Co-own any failures	Rarely are there just lessons to be learned on one side only; chances are both the provider and customer have adjustments to make	
Don't assume priorities are known or shared	Don't assume that just because you work in the same organization, your partner already understands your priorities. They may have no knowledge or appreciation of the work that you do outside your relationship with them.	Don't assume that just because you work in the same organization, your partner understands your priorities already. Realize you aren't their only priority: know how your request fits into overall workflow and workload.

ESSENTIAL #1 | START WITH PARTNERSHIPS

INVESTMENT #6: ADVOCATE

Remember the role that Rosa and Gianna played for each other? Rosa was Gianna's advocate to the manufacturing team, and Gianna provided an additional voice from Rosa's team to corporate. Being an advocate means you are their eyes and ears, ambassador and supporter, and they are yours—you go above and beyond mere helping and appreciating or being a good team player:

Good Team Players...	Good Partners...
Help out when asked	See when their help is needed and jump in
Solve a problem that is brought to them	See problems and bring them to light for their partner
Thank partners for a great job	Let others know what an outstanding partner they are
Let partners know when things aren't going quite right	Help partners figure out how to fix a problem

The right-hand column outlines some behaviors that have the potential to compound investments in terms of the trust between two partners. Advocating is much more proactive than other partnership behaviors and much more hands-on, which is what makes it more risky but infinitely more potent. It is nearly impossible not to want to partner with someone who is your advocate.

INVESTMENT #7: INCLUDE

I conducted a number of focus groups for a client looking to understand how they could increase the partnership level with their distributors. They had made a concerted effort over the previous 12 months to communicate better with distributors, but still felt that they were disconnected. After talking to 50+ distributors, the answer was simple—in fact, so simple that the corporate staff questioned my results. The distributors wanted to be included. They wanted to be included in decisions, brought into problem solving. The corporate staff had increased the information going out, so the distributors were informed—but that only got them so far (to the Transactional Partnership level). For the distributors, information wasn't enough. The corporate team needed to compound its investment—they needed to include.

Including people in meetings, involving them in decisions and problem solving and sharing information tells them you not only trust them, you value them. And the bonus is that this inclusion will also improve the quality of those meetings and decisions.

Pulling Back: When Your Partnership Overreaches

Usually the business requires a more advanced partnership than the two partners are exhibiting, but there can be times where your level of partnership actually exceeds requirements. This may not seem like a bad thing, but here's what you should look out for:

- How do others see it? Do they view the partnership as favoritism? Does it make them question your motives?

- Are you using your energy wisely? Is the energy better spent on partnerships that more closely align with business needs?

- Does overshooting the partnership lead you down the wrong path? Is this partner more influential than he or she should be in terms of how you get results?

We all have our version of A Tale of Two Partners. At any given time we will have partnerships that cover the continuum from new or Dysfunctional to Integrated. Fit matters. So does your mindset. And whether measured by small

To successfully solve a problem, view it at the enterprise level, not your personal silo level.

ZOOM OUT

deposits or significant investments, change in a partnership starts with you.

A wise practitioner who was interviewed for this book put it best: "You only know what people are willing to let you see." With strong partnerships, you will be allowed to see more, and that line of sight will help you with the three biggest challenges (covered in the next three chapters): goal alignment, role clarity and decision-making.

IN SUMMARY

EMBRACE

→ Partnerships are the way work gets done in matrix roles.

→ Many people are involved in your work: let them in. Don't spend energy blocking them out.

→ Partnerships require increasing investments in trust, communication and constructive conflict.

→ Don't wait for your partner to change or initiate the change—it's up to you.

→ Be deliberate in your efforts to build, maintain and repair partnerships.

WHERE TO START

→ Take a critical look at who you should be partnering with. Start by looking at how your role is structured and identify who is key in each of your areas of responsibility.

→ Assess the level of your key partnerships. What does the business call for? Is the partnership up to the task? Do both of you agree on the business need behind the partnership and the partnership level that is called for?

→ Invest in one or two of your key partnerships over the next three weeks. See how the dynamics shift.

IN PRACTICE

FOR LEADERS

In matrix organizations, your partnerships are not your own. Your partnerships clear the path for partnership between your teams and other teams; the trust people have in you extends to your team. You have an especially important role in the partnerships that are formed on your team, and your partnerships clear the path for those that work for you. Emphasize, encourage, coach and reward partnering behaviors. If you share or "co-manage" employees with another leader, put forth deliberate effort to build the partnership with your co-manager so that the employee never feels pulled or "in the middle." Your partnerships with your co-manager drives the co-managed employees' success.

FOR CROSS-FUNCTIONAL/MATRIX TEAMS

The level of partnership required between you and other team members will vary—most will be Collaborative, but you may have a few that are Transactional or Integrated. Don't expect or work toward having equal partnerships with all—it simply isn't needed. Be very honest and open about talking about the level at which you should be operating. The partnerships between individual team members and individuals outside the team matter. Talk about them openly and strategize about who and how to build partnerships with these stakeholders.

WORKING VIRTUALLY

Left to their own devices, virtual partnerships will turn transactional. You will need to fight this default. All investments apply, but the level of deliberate effort increases exponentially and will take time. You will never find time to build partnerships; you have to make time and deliberately connect. Find simple ways: log into your calls 2 minutes early or stay 2 minutes late and initiate conversation outside the task either verbally or through chat. This mimics the pre- and post-meeting chatter that happens when you are physically together. Be on video, camera on as close to 100% as possible. Acknowledge the challenge with others and reach out for 10-minute catch-ups, grab a virtual cup of coffee, reserve an hour a week for "office hours" where anyone can call spontaneously for a quick chat. You will have to structure the informal into your daily practice (as diametrically opposed as that sounds).

> *"Every day you spend drifting away from your goals is a waste not only of that day, but also the additional day it takes to regain lost ground."*
>
> RALPH MARSTON

ESSENTIAL #2

GET GOALS ALIGNED

You have to start with **PARTNERSHIPS** to get...

GOALS ALIGNED
ROLES CLEAR
DECISIONS MADE

All of this requires you to...

FLEX YOUR INFLUENCE MUSCLE
COMMUNICATE WITHOUT ASSUMPTION
TREAT MEETINGS LIKE THEY MATTER

WHAT IT IS

When working cross-functionally, misalignments are unavoidable—sometimes even intentional. To master the matrix you must be artful in bringing together those misalignments with the potential to be constructive, while also vigilant in identifying and resolving conflicts with the potential to derail.

WHAT THE RESEARCH SAYS

What's most important:
» Seeing the bigger-picture goals beyond your own goals and needs

What's most likely to trip you up:
» Staying focused on a limited number of goals

$J$$I$$M$ is a marketing director, and one of his roles involves leading a cross-functional team that drives a complex, ongoing approval process involving Sales, Marketing, R&D, Legal and several scientific functions. This eight-person team—representing each of the eight functions in the process—is charged with approving promotional material that must be scientifically exact, legally sound, in accordance with all regulatory requirements, aligned with the marketing strategy and, ultimately, effectively sell the product. Each representative on the team has a different idea of what makes "good" promotional material and a different goal regarding what the material needs to be. The perfect promotional material from a legal perspective makes no sense to a marketer. Left to their devices, sales would throw in anything that might lead to a sale, and the scientists would come up with promotional content that made sense only to them. Eight different goals, eight different agendas—an eight-way intersection with Jim in the middle serving as traffic cop meant endless meetings and an approval time that was measured in months.

Johanna is a director of Finance, with a solid line reporting relationship to Marcia, the VP of Finance for her division, and a dotted line reporting relationship to Kenan, the VP of Manufacturing for the division. It is May; five months into the fiscal year, and things are humming along as planned for Johanna and her team. Then Kenan stops by and informs Johanna that one of his top goals for the year requires some fairly detailed, customized financial reports. He will need Johanna and her team to design them and provide them on a monthly basis, perhaps weekly basis, beginning next month. As Kenan is talking, Johanna is acutely aware of the Finance function's Top Five Goals, which are posted on the bulletin board in her office. On the top of that list is the goal to standardize all financial reports globally. A goal of standardization and a goal requiring customization: which one will win out?

Competing goals was the #1 challenge reported by matrix practitioners.

SURVEY

If you have been in a matrix role for a period of time, you have faced competing goals like Jim and Johanna. In fact competing goals was the #1 challenge identified by the matrix managers who took part in the research for this book.

The Two Types of Matrix Goal Misalignments

As we've already talked about, organizations want the best of both worlds, so they set up teams and reporting relationships that bring different sides together to produce solutions that benefit the enterprise as a whole. In part, misalignments are common because matrix roles exist to create goal collisions. This is the type of misalignment that Jim's team faced every day. The organization didn't want a solution based on the goals of only one function, but for the organization as a whole. It wanted a solution that achieved the goals of Sales *and* Marketing *and* Legal, etc.—thus the cross-functional team.

Natural misalignments are not the only goal clashes prevalent in matrix roles. Because these roles exist in complex organizations and operate within multiple matrices, misalignments also occur because we forget to communicate, assume alignment or let goals drift until they collide. I call these *human-made* misalignments. This is the dilemma Johanna was faced with. She was in a matrix role because the organization didn't want a finance team that focused exclusively on technical expertise or one engulfed by the business it supported. It wanted a team that was technically adept *and* steeped in the realities of the business—thus the dual-reporting relationship. But in this case, the connection between the two parts of the matrix was frayed, goals drifted, and a misalignment was created.

"One half of knowing what you want is knowing what you must give up before you get it."

SIDNEY HOWARD

Behind each dispute lies significant time and effort—spent by already stretched resources—to realign and reprioritize. Whether natural or human made, unless you work through misalignments, you and your partners will be paddling in two different directions: you'll end up exhausted, but in the same place. And "in the same place" is definitely not where anyone wants to land at milestone time.

Four Ground Rules for Goal Alignment

Four basic ground rules in goal alignment can help you whether you are tackling a goal conflict that is inherent to your matrix role or one that sprouted up while no one was looking.

IT'S BIGGER THAN YOU

I use a great exercise with matrix teams that pits the goals of two people against the goals of everyone else in the room. The details aren't important, but suffice it to say that throughout the game, participants must choose between options that earn the most points for their pair and options that earn the most points for the whole group (usually four pairs) but mean less for their individual pair. What participants don't realize until the end is that every individual pair will maximize their own points if they all consistently choose the option that earns the most points for the whole group. Having run this exercise dozens of times, it is clear that our natural inclination is to do what is right for our pair. Whether based on proximity (each pair sits together, about 6–8 feet from the others) or the fact that it is easier to align with one other person than 7, our natural inclination is to think small and immediate. We tend to define "team" rather narrowly, and when we don't zoom out we tend to become very competitive.

In a matrix role there is always an overarching goal—bigger than you, sometimes even bigger than your team, function or geography—that takes precedence over any individual goals. If you go in determined to maximize your personal success or your immediate team's success, the matrix breaks down. There is an "and," not an "or," at the heart of every cross-functional goal—forgetting or ignoring this will lead to suboptimal results as well as suboptimal relationships.

You have to look broadly to see the "and" at the heart of every matrix goal.

ZOOM OUT

BE REALISTIC

Google "optimism and goals," and you will find thousands (if not millions) of studies and blogs touting the benefits of optimism in setting and achieving goals. Dig a little deeper and you will find that when it comes to competing goals, highly optimistic people tend to push forward on the competing goals (sometimes doggedly so) versus resolving the conflict by giving up or reducing their commitment to one of the goals (Canto and Blanton, 1999). All that sounds good and sounds like persistence, but I see matrix practitioners every day struggling with this—driven, optimistic and much more willing to hit the "add" than the

Be realistic about the degree to which you can/ should chase after competing goals.

MINDSET

"subtract" on the goal calculator. Individuals, teams and organizations have got to be more realistic on goals and must be willing to make difficult choices when working cross-functionally because these conflicts expand exponentially when working across functions. And the difficult choices have to be real choices, not deferment, as one client organization I work with is struggling with—their tough choices are less about "no" and most like "not now," which just means you have a whole lot of possible priorities floating around and distracting.

BE READY TO MAKE TRADE-OFFS

Without willingness to make trade-offs, an intersection team like Jim's is doomed to fail. They need to keep in mind that the situation is "bigger than them," and maintaining a good dose of realism is necessary for the next step—trade-offs.

There will absolutely be compromises, some (perhaps many) that you will have to make yourself. Going into a conflict assuming that trade-offs will take place automatically shifts into what you say and how you say it, and this change can't help but shift outcomes. Not only will your willingness to make trade-offs shift the outcome of the discussion at hand, but future disputes as well. Making a trade-off has the potential to loosen others up—psychologically, most people will feel the need to repay in kind.

Making a trade-off has the potential to loosen others up—psychologically, most people will feel the need to repay in kind.

JUJITSU

ASSUME NOTHING

Operating at high speed, Johanna didn't slow down to make sure she and Kenan were in sync on annual goals. And Kenan assumed that any goal of his was Johanna's as well. These assumptions helped them pick up speed, but tripped them up in the end. The ambiguity that surrounds matrix roles and the speed at which we work leads us to rely on assumptions—they function as shortcuts. However, these assumptions are the main ingredient for goal misalignments, when, for example, we assume that others know our goals, assume that our priority is their priority or assume that goals aligned at the beginning of the year are still aligned seven months later. Assume nothing. If your matrix is above you, don't assume your bosses are aligned. When working cross-functionally, don't assume your goal or priority is shared by others. Ask questions, share information and clarify. Essential #6 covers assumptions in communication in full, in all matrix contexts, but it holds a special place in goal alignment.

Align from the Start and Then Realign as You Go

Jim and Johanna share a common need to align with their matrix partners right from the start. For Jim, whose team is set up to collide, his goal is to cultivate these perspectives into work products that maximize the organization effectively and efficiently. Aligning from the start will help this team find common ground, so they can better cultivate the conflicts that really matter.

For Johanna, her misalignment happened because wires were crossed, or maybe things shifted and the owners of the goals didn't think to realign with stakeholders. Someone took their eye off the ball, got caught up in their part of the world and didn't look up to see who needed to be aligned around their goal. For Johanna, aligning from the start will help *prevent* misalignments.

Alignment begins with setting goals and relies on sticking to a finite number of goals that are kept in the forefront. As one leader who took part in the research for this book put simply, "You must have a huge focus on a few things." There are three requirements that set the foundation for goal alignment in matrix roles: include the right people, land on a limited set of goals and keep goals in the foreground. You must have all three to ensure alignment. Here's what happens when you don't:

Include the right People	Land on a limited set of goals	Keep goals in the foreground	Results:
✓	✓	✓	GOAL ALIGNMENT
✓	✓		Distractions, drifting
✓		✓	Diffused efforts
	✓	✓	Stakeholder resistance

INCLUDE THE RIGHT PEOPLE

Remember Mary and Fran in The Tale of Two Partnerships? They had given up including and started just throwing goals and decisions over the fence at each other. With every missed opportunity for inclusion, resentment built up and trust faded. What they were missing was the fact that when you set up goals with the help of those people who will actually support them or have a stake in them, the goals are always going to be more realistic and better understood. You will also be developing goals that people actually feel some ownership over. These goals stand a decent chance of survival in ever-changing multidimensional organizations. Goals set behind closed doors, with just those in your sandbox or silo, risk diminished relevance and practicality, not to mention resentment when people believe they were excluded, forgotten or discounted.

The ideal situation for setting goals involves having all interested parties in the room, but that's rarely possible due to timing, geography and other practicalities. Start by identifying the key people to involve. There are probably more than you think. For example, if you are setting goals for a cross-functional team, including your team members is obvious. But what about their solid line bosses? Don't miss an opportunity to build their understanding and showcase their support for the project. In any event, identify the key people and push to have a few others. Those who you can't get in the room can be involved in another way—ask them to be a sounding board or a reviewer.

There are probably more people to include in goal setting than you think. **ZOOM OUT**

Let participants know how they will be used—are they giving you input so you can set the goals? Or are you bringing the group in to reach consensus on the goals? There is a big difference between these two purposes, and you need to let them know which type it is up front.

Your goal-setting process needs to be inclusive, as does your goal communication process. There will be people who need to know your goals because they impact their own goals. If you have levels beneath you, your goals will need to be cascaded so that others can identify the priorities and feed their goals into yours. Think of any others in your cross-functional environment who should know about your goals—especially people who you may need to pull in or hand off to.

LAND ON A LIMITED SET OF GOALS

Select, restricted, limited. These are all good words to describe the goals you set for yourself or your matrix team. I don't recommend a specific number of goals, because whenever I was asked in the past, organizations ran with whatever magic number I mentioned. The problem was that they didn't truly go out and create, say, 5 great goals. They simply tried to roll 50 goals into 5. What I can tell you is, the ideal number is a heck of a lot smaller than you think.

Maintaining alignment across your matrix is impossible with a laundry list of goals. If you want tight alignment and maximum focus, decrease the number of goals you have to pursue. The number of

"The pessimist complains about the wind; the optimist expects it to change; the realist adjusts the sails."

WILLIAM ARTHUR WARD

goals you create at the beginning of the year correlates to the conversation you have at the end of the year. The fewer goals, the more likely your conversation revolves around how much you accomplished. The more goals, the more likely your conversation focuses on how much you didn't finish and how many you just plain forgot about. I have yet to work with a client who at the end of the year said they didn't set enough goals at the beginning of the year.

How do you get to a handful? Stack them. Create criteria based on the highest-level goals and strategies of the organization and rank them. Be brutal, and apply that brutality to determine your threshold. Above the line is in the mix, below the line falls out (but save the list for next year—this is your starting point). Then hang on to those rankings—you will use them all year to make tough calls about what you or your team does. Alternatively, you can use an ABC prioritization (A=must have; B=need to have; C=nice to have), *if* you have parameters on how many (or what percent) you will have in each category. Without these limits, everything becomes an A priority. Whatever you do, compare goals to each other, not just to your criteria, and force yourself to make difficult choices.

One last rationale for keeping a limited, memorable list of goals when there are too many goals to remember, people will default to the ones that are most obvious. And guess what? The ones that are most obvious are the ones most within their lane—and then you have fallen out of the traffic circle, zoomed-out, cross-functional mindset.

Finally, test your list with a few independent, objective outsiders—people completely outside of the process who will not be involved in executing the goals. Walk them through your criteria, your list and the rationale for your rankings or ratings. These bystanders can match goals directly to criteria, not through the filter of history, politics or emotions.

KEEP GOALS IN THE FOREGROUND

"Out of sight out of mind" is the reality for many goals set with high expectations in a conference room at the beginning of the year. It is even more so for the goals that criss-cross yours. Chances are Kenan—Johanna's partner who was unknowingly declaring war on Johanna's functional goals—heard something about some Finance goal in January, but didn't hear about it again and forgot when he went all in on his own initiative. Once you have set the goals, the real work begins—not just in working toward the goals, but in keeping focused. If you have picked a limited number of meaningful goals, this shouldn't be hard. If you have picked too many or they lack relevance, your focus is sure to wander before the ink is dry on your goal document.

Keeping goals in the foreground helps prevent the drift and shift that leads to slipping back into silo thinking, "what's right for me." For one team I worked with, the collective goal boiled down to a one word mantra: *vanilla*. They were working on a cloud-based ERP system and every time someone started down the path of "my function needs the system to be customized to do blah, blah, blah" the group reminded them that their target was *vanilla*—a plain, noncustomized system that could be easily supported by the vendor. They kept that collective goal in the forefront by constantly reminding themselves of it.

Here are three very simple ways to keep goals in the foreground:

1. **Make goals visible to everyone.** In the example above, *vanilla* was a verbal reminder, but physical reminders can be equally powerful. Bulletin boards, white boards, screen savers, shared drives, collaboration sites, posters, laminated cards, tattoos, whatever it takes. And in whatever form—scorecards, list, spreadsheets. Don't bury your goals in the shared drive. Keep your goals and your progress visible—doing this shows that you are serious about the goal; it isn't going away and "Hey look, we are actually getting traction on this."

2. **Use goals to filter priorities.** Goals should be used to drive actions and decisions on what work should be done and when. I can't say this any clearer than Gene, a project lead on a large global initiative:

> *"In the team meetings I remind everyone, 'What you're working on should be driving to one of these goals, and if it's not you should be having a conversation with me or your manager about it. We need to make sure that at the end of the year we can look back and say number one, we did everything we needed to do to achieve the goals that have been set out either for you individually or for us as a team. Two, anything that we did that didn't support those goals was a justified, conscious decision.'"*

Pamela, an R&D project manager in a large multinational pharmaceuticals company, tells a similar story on a larger scale:

> *"It sounds really simplistic, but we have a ranked list from number one to however many projects are going on at that time. Everyone has access to this information, and it is updated at least quarterly. So if you are working on #4 and someone comes in and asks you to drop everything for number #14, your response is pretty obvious. That doesn't mean you don't talk about it, but 9 times out of 10 you end up sticking with #4 and the conversation is pretty short."*

3. **Use goals as a framework.** Your goals are not just a reference, but also an organizing framework for the year. All meetings, whether they are informal one-on-ones, monthly team meetings or large quarterly town halls, should have an agenda structured around the goals and outcomes focused on the goals. Everything you do and communicate should be structured around the same few goals.

I have a client whose super power is the three suggestions listed above; he is laser focused on making sure his organization is aware and aligned. His townhalls are a work of goal alignment art—a constant drum beat of key strategies and related goals and progress against measures. At first, he worried people would tire of his message, so he asked me to check in with his team and extended team. Bored? No way. They loved the focus and the predictability and they really loved seeing progress. The cadence helped bring a calm clarity to a very large, very complex and ambiguous global company.

New goals and realities will always come up, and when goals must shift, make sure you shift them purposefully. Don't just let them drift and assume everyone is following the drift. Be as conscious about resetting goals as you were about setting them in the first place. Communicate the shift broadly so that people can adjust their individual goals and priorities. Also prepare yourself for people's responses. Some will take the change in stride; others will question it. One of the leaders I talked to described goal realignment as feeling "like your base just became unsteady; like your foundation just moved under your feet." Be ready to support your team through the shift.

The guidelines here are your starting point, but no amount of pre-alignment is going to eliminate collisions. To be effective in truly managing matrix goals, you have to be very adept at **channeling and cultivating** the inherent conflicts into solutions that maximize the big picture goal, **preventing** those conflicts that are caused by neglect and, for those that slip past you, **resolving** through your own devices or other's.

Channeling and Cultivating Natural Misalignments

Let's go back to Jim, the traffic cop in a cross-functional team's eight-way intersection. There were actually multiple "Jims" in this organization, a total of five teams with this same configuration and end goal. I observed all of them in an effort to help them "manage conflict better." If you have been paying attention so far, you know that these teams were the nucleus of naturally occurring and purposeful goal collision. They didn't need to "manage" conflict—they needed to channel it in a way that helped them reach their collective goal more effectively and efficiently.

Some teams were better than others, and one team really stood out. Here's what that team did differently:

- They didn't personalize the conflict. They didn't attack the opinions of others or feel the need to defend their own. They channeled their disagreements toward their desired end.

- They constantly went back to the big picture through a simple mantra of "scientifically sound, won't get us thrown in jail and still sells the product." Not just the team leader, but team members always reframed things. When they got stuck, they went back to the mantra; when an individual was having a hard time selling beyond their lane, the mantra came out.

- They took each other's perspective. The marketing person asked legal questions; the regulatory rep brought up clinical issues. It was hard for me to tell who came from which function—they were all concerned with coming up with solutions that made sense from all angles.

- They used their trump cards (flat out disagreement) wisely and sparingly. Because they conserved these, it packed a powerful punch when they put their foot down.

- When a team member refuted something, they had a follow-up suggestion. They focused on what could be done and what possible options were available.

- They got everything on the table. If a perspective wasn't coming out, they asked the person or someone else offered it up.

The team leader made sure there was time set aside to hear everyone's perspectives and modeled the desired behaviors. It was clear that everyone shared his mindset. When I asked the team leader what he did, he said some of their "ground rules" were set up formally, but most were just based on having the right people on the team to model behaviors and the others following suit. In his words, "Those who have a different definition of 'team' pretty much stick out like a sore thumb."

To use the language from Essential #1—this team was clearly a group of

Integrated Partners. They had learned not only to deal with conflict, but to actually use it to their advantage in delivering their work product. But here's where the genius of the team leader really became evident. Not only did team members have strong partnerships with the lead and each other, but the team leader had strong relationships with what I call the "outer circle"—the managers of the team members:

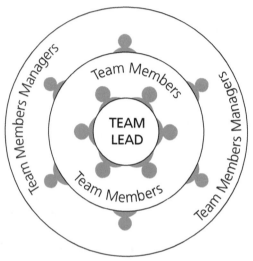

Once I saw this team and their mindsets and practices, I never looked at natural misalignments the same. Since then I have seen different varieties of these approaches practiced by teams and individuals in the middle of complex junctures of goals—they are able to keep themselves from getting tied up in cross-functional knots through partnerships, zooming out, solution mindset and honest up-front communication.

This allowed the lead to be involved in selection of team members and maintain the team's empowerment by pushing back when the members' managers attempted to veto a team decision. This partnership connect was vital in making this team work.

Preventing Human-Made Goal Misalignments

Now we return to Johanna, stuck between two goals: standardization of process and customization of reports. Both she and Kenan, her dotted line supervisor, were carrying around assumptions about their goals and either didn't align at the beginning or didn't check in with each other later to make sure they were still aligned.

Here's what she could have done to *prevent* the goal conflict:

Make the hunt for misalignments everyone's job: Individuals in matrix positions are the recipients of goals/priorities from other parts of the organization, and as such, have a unique point of view. Often they are the only ones who see misalignments that are occurring or about to occur. As one leader put it, if you are in a matrix role, you have to "be on the hunt" for priorities that conflict, goals that collide and timelines that clash. Furthermore, you have to be willing to bring these up. As a team leader, you have to make it clear that transparency is key and that calling attention to competing goals is not only OK but necessary for problem solving.

Create a forum: Even in a matrix role, you can't see all sides; alignments can only be found through dialogue with your bosses, team and peers. Create a forum for this and do it on a regular basis. Maybe it will take place at the end of each weekly meeting or at the end of a one to one—whatever it looks like, make it a practice to bring up misalignments and ask others about what they are seeing. Ask questions: Is there any new information that would lead to a misalignment? New projects or initiatives that have been added? Timelines that are changing? This constant scanning catches misalignments before they crash and turn ugly. Dealing with conflicts as they approach is easier and less emotional than waiting until they're right in front of you.

Look for early warning signs: What are some signs that goals are starting to drift for someone in your matrix? Maybe they miss meetings or start delegating the meetings to someone else, or their response time extends. These signs should tell you that something else is drawing their attention away. When attention strays, goals drift. When you see an early warning sign, bring it up directly to the person. Start with, "I noticed…" Get an understanding of what is pulling them. Reiterate the importance of the goal and address how you can get things back on track.

The bottom line is, to get good at navigating goal misalignments, you must *anticipate and normalize them.* They will absolutely occur, and if you have that mindset, they don't throw you off, they frustrate you less and you move through them with a completely different level of ease.

Anticipate goal alignments to navigate with more ease.

MINDSET

Resolving Human-Made Misalignments: Pick Your Battles

When a misalignment manages to evade early detection, like Johanna and Kenan's, you have some choices for how to resolve it. In the introduction we introduced a building block called "Triage." Here's what triage looks like in goal alignment (re-

Pick your battles based on timeframe and impact.

TRIAGE

member, if you are highly optimistic then the light section labeled "let it go" is going to be large for you and you may try to ignore the misalignments believing you can "do it all." This is not sustainable.):

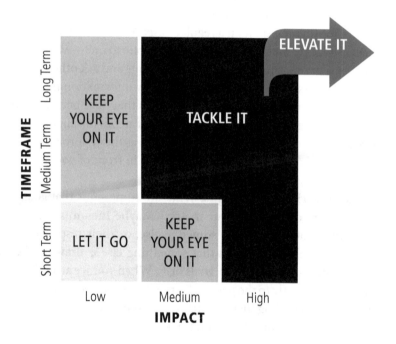

You have to consider impact and timeframe. If a goal conflict doesn't have a big impact on you or the team, just let it go and carry the conflict—work both goals. The bigger the impact and the longer it will stay in conflict, the more likely you are to need to directly resolve it. For the really big issues, you may attempt to resolve, but if that fails your back-up strategy may be to elevate to a person with more influence or authority.

Partnership-Driven Resolution

In the case of Johanna and Kenan, which is a true story from an interview, here's how the conflict played out:

> *Once I realized Kenan's expectations and the collision course they were on with Finance's goals, I considered my options. Kenan is a pretty persuasive guy, and the easy thing would have been to just have my team jump in and start designing and producing the reports for him. We would have looked like heroes to Manufacturing, but would have been scolded by the Finance function. Or I could have taken it to my boss and had him deal with it, which would have really made Kenan mad. Or I could have launched into my well-rehearsed spiel about the importance of the Finance function's vision of "one financial report globally," which Kenan cares nothing about and which would have built up resentment between the two functions.*
>
> *I ended up just asking a lot of questions. I wanted to get a clear understanding of what he needed. I knew his business well, so I could push a little and say things like, "Are you sure that is what you need, because here's what I have seen you use." I came out of this with a really good sense of his needs—I think he even understood his needs better. Then I laid the Finance goal on the table. And I basically turned to him and said, "This is where I am being pulled. I can easily get you this and this, but this is outside the parameters of what the Finance function is asking me to do. Can you live with this so that I can do what is right for both functions?" We have a good relationship, and he's been in a matrix role before, so that helped, but in the end I was able to give him the 85% of what he wanted that lined up with Finance's goals, and he learned to live without the other 15%.*

Johanna and Kenan recovered nicely—their steps toward resolution were much better than their preventative measures. Here's what Johanna and Kenan did right:

Don't just "take the mountain." Johanna didn't just take Kenan's request at face value and run with it. Had she tried to hold both goals, she would have ended up failing on at least one of them, and the trust and credibility of her team would have been shot.

Ask questions to clarify. Because Johanna paused and didn't just take the mountain, she was able to ask questions to make sure she understood Kenan's goal, if/how it collided with hers, and eventually that information led to a solution that made sense for both of them. What is important to remember here is that *when you think you have the full picture, ask more questions.* What sounds like a misalignment may not be when you really dig into the request. Sometimes clarification, not resolution, is what a situation calls for. At the very least you will have a much clearer sense of what and where the disconnect is, which will help you choose a tactic for resolution.

Consider your options. Again, because Johanna paused and used that opportunity to learn more about the misalignment, she was able to think through her options. She didn't just take the mountain, but she didn't automatically elevate it to her boss either. Both of those are easy, short-term fixes. She chose the tougher but ultimately more rewarding path—attempting to resolve the misalignment with a real solution, not just by delaying the pain.

Rules of Elevation

In both natural and human-made goal conflicts, there is always the option to elevate the goal conflict to a level above you. This alternative should be used after trying to resolve the conflict, not as your go-to first step.

Note that elevation is different from asking for advice or giving a heads-up. Asking your boss for advice on tackling a goal alignment issue makes sense regardless of the situation. Giving a heads-up to your boss might also make sense if he or she is going to hear about it or be asked about the conversation. If you are approaching a person in your matrix or on your team, you may want to pull in their supervisor, depending on your relationship with both players and the nature of the issue. They may be able to advise you, clarify things, or you may need them to reinforce the message after the discussion.

Elevation takes things a step further and really lays the issue in another person's lap—like Johanna's option to bring the conflict with Kenan to her boss. You don't want to overplay this card—the risk is twofold. First, you risk perceptions of

Elevate with the full picture, not just your perspective.

ZOOM OUT

dependence—not being willing or able to resolve things on your own. Second, you could be accused of overdramatizing the situation. The more you elevate problems, the less potent elevation becomes and the more you look powerless.

In a matrix role, it may also be unclear whom to elevate a conflict to. It could be your boss, a team member's boss, a stakeholder's boss or all of the above. It could be the boss who sits where the matrix merges. One of the leaders I interviewed called this person "The Lowest Common Boss." Depending on how high up you have to go to find this person, he or she may be an option, but if the Lowest Common Boss is more than two levels above you, think twice.

Regardless of whom you elevate to, when you elevate, you need to have the full picture—not just your piece of the picture. The minute you elevate with just one side of the story, you have lost all credibility. Go back to your mindset—it's bigger than you.

A few tips on elevating a goal conflict:

Don't ever cry wolf. Make sure you have done your homework and you have all the facts pointing to a misalignment. Don't send the person you are elevating to on a wild goose chase for a misalignment that doesn't exist.

Be objective. Present the misalignment from both sides.

Frame it in a larger context. Describe the misalignment in a larger context—not how it affects you, but how it affects team and organizational goals.

Provide your ideas on steps to resolution. Do not just place the problem in their lap; have a proposal for what to do next and all the information needed to take that next step.

A Note on Goal Alignment and Rewards

As you will recall from the Introduction, there are a few showstoppers in matrix roles, and one is reward. Goals are usually connected to rewards. If you are up against a competing goal with a reward linked to it that is bigger than the reward linked to yours, realize that you are limited in what you can make happen. These types of conflicts have to be brought to light—the project is set up to fail, and you will have to be unrelenting in drawing attention to this disconnect.

The same is true if you feel a personal pull based on rewards. There will absolutely be times when goals conflict, you are stuck in the middle and the goal initiated from the side of the matrix that pays you will feel like the stronger pull. Again, these types of conflicts have to be brought to light—you are in a no-win situation and have to be unrelenting in drawing attention to this disconnect.

Alignment is a point in time. You have it momentarily, and you fight for it continuously. Like every Essential in this book, alignment doesn't grow organically, it needs tending. Goal misalignment is one of the biggest time wasters in matrix roles. Being good at preventing, anticipating and resolving goal conflicts frees up your time and your team's time to work constructively toward milestones. Resolving misalignments with your bosses will makes your life easier and ensure that your efforts are exerted in the correct direction, not wasted.

IN SUMMARY

EMBRACE

→ Goal conflicts as an intended consequence of the matrix and leverage this to get optimal solutions.

→ Your responsibility to prevent human-made conflicts—don't let goals drift and shift

→ Inclusive goal setting to drive alignment from the beginning

→ Vigilance in looking for misalignments and tackling them when it makes sense

TRY

→ Get brutal with selecting goals by evaluating and stacking them against each other

→ Once goals are set, keep them visible and use them as a framework for meetings and to prioritize work

→ Be on the hunt for misalignments; have a forum for identifying and resolving goal conflicts

→ When you identify a misalignment, pause long enough to ask questions and understand the nature of the issue before you either pursue both goals or resolve the conflict

→ Follow the ground rules for matrix goal alignment: always go back to the bigger-picture goal; be realistic in when you can pursue dual goals; be ready to make trade-offs and assume nothing about your partners' understanding of and engagement in your goals

IN PRACTICE

FOR LEADERS

Don't allow endless elevation. The ambiguity of matrix roles causes some people to throw up their hands and just elevate all goal misalignments to you. Although it might feel momentarily good to solve their problem, don't take the bait. Set ground rules on what and when to elevate. Make it clear that they don't have a blank check on this. One leader I worked with gives his team a "six shooter." They have six opportunities per year for elevation, and he advises that they hold at least a few until the 4th quarter, because that's usually when the scramble starts and things need to get settled.

Stay disciplined and focused. Establish a solid drum beat of a repeated message on what is important. That doesn't mean you don't shift or can't be agile. It just means that the shifts are conscious, transparent and with communicated rationale.

Build strong partnerships across the organization. These partnerships will facilitate communication (to mitigate human-made misalignments), and the inherent trust will make channeling natural misalignments much, much easier.

FOR CROSS-FUNCTIONAL/MATRIX TEAMS

This is at the heart of what a cross-functional team is built on. If you aren't able to navigate goal misalignments, you won't be able to get decisions made.

- Take off your team jersey—it's not about what aligns best with your function, it's about what is right for the overall team objective
- When stuck, step back to see the overall goal
- Don't fall on your sword for every decision that isn't in line with the goals, needs, priorities or opinions of your "home" function—triage.
- When you have to say "no" to something that isn't in line with your home function's goals, needs, priorities or opinions, follow it with a related idea ("that approach isn't in alignment with the standards in place, but here's a similar way to consider that is...").

WORKING VIRTUALLY

Virtual cross-functional work requires next-level discipline and communication. The use of goals as a framework for every interaction (one on ones to team meetings to townhalls) is imperative. I have found that visual representation that is repeated helps as well—one slide, one diagram that you keep going back, to stay aligned. Build extra time to sort out misalignments. Virtual communication just takes more frequency, because the interactions are (and should be) broken up into smaller increments. Anticipate this. And, it cannot be overstated—focus on building partners. They are harder to build but even more important virtually.

*"We do not grow by knowing
all of the answers, but rather by
living with the questions."*

MAX DE PREE

ESSENTIAL #3
CLARIFY ROLES

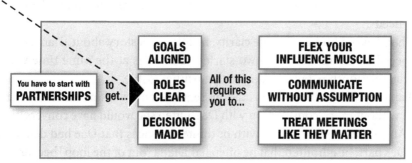

WHAT IT IS

Boundaries can blur in matrix roles. The key to understanding roles is to define them without expecting total clarity, then get comfortable with what isn't clear. Accept roles as they are; build trust to fill gaps in clarity.

WHAT THE RESEARCH SAYS

What's important:
» Knowing what your role in the organization is

What will likely trip you up:
» Resolving role clarity issues so the team/project roles are clear to others.

DAE is a director of Finance for a technology company. His matrix role is best described as an internal customer hub. He is the lead Finance person for a small business unit and acts as a general contractor—he is the point person for the business with a dotted line to Angel, the General Manager. He relies on a web of specialists in the Finance function to deliver on client needs.

When I asked him about role clarity, he told me a story about Diana, one of the specialists in his web. The two started their roles at the same time with a collegial relationship, but it was quickly turning hostile.

Diana seemed to throw information, requests and work products "over the fence" without much consultation with Dae. Often she would have conversations with Angel that would conflict with or dilute messages that Dae had delivered. For Dae's part, he admitted that he often left Diana "out of the loop" because she was in a building across the campus. Sometimes he felt like he didn't have time to fill her in on what was happening with the client.

This could have continued, with each infraction fortifying the walls of their individual silos, while Angel and his team paid the price. But Dae did something that I found matrix masters do a lot of. He took a step back to diagnose the problem and figure out what was within his control to address. Dae had felt for some time that their roles could be clearer. What he didn't know was that this lack of role clarity was leading to behaviors that were eroding trust between the two of them.

The division was preparing for the annual budgeting process. It was an intense, highly visible, three-month process for the division, and Diana was Dae's partner. Dae knew the relationship with Diana was on a crash course, and the partnership required for the initiative could be the breaking point for them.

He suggested that he and Diana work together to define each task in the budgeting process and identify who would do what for each task—who would take the lead, who would provide input and what they needed to keep each other informed of. They completed this outline and shared it with Angel so he knew what to expect from each of them.

They followed the role outline for the next three months with very few issues. They referred back to it on occasion to make sure they were on track and clear on their responsibilities. The process went smoothly—hand-offs were made, each stepped up when they needed to and stepped back when it was appropriate.

As a byproduct of using this structured approach to defining their roles, trust between Diana and Dae increased. Because expectations were clear, there was no more "throwing things over the wall"—Diana knew when to consult Dae and vice-versa. Because communication needs were unambiguous, they both felt well informed, which in turn helped them to rebuild trust. The success of this process helped make day-to-day tasks, which didn't have full, formal role documentation, much less taxing.

Dae estimated it took three hours to create the role document. I asked him how much time it saved, and he responded, "Immeasurable, because it didn't just save me time on this project, it saved me time and energy on all subsequent work I did with Diana. The work flows easily now, and the increased trust allowed us to move much, much faster."

The reasons behind Dae and Diana's frustrations are typical in matrix roles, as are the ramifications. In matrix roles, interdependencies increase and can become a web of converging, diverging, overlapping and parallel roles. Understanding who occupies this web and what their roles are is central to getting results.

In researching this book, I asked people what they thought was most difficult about matrix roles. Over a third of their top challenges tied back to role clarity. For example, accountability was often mentioned. When roles aren't defined, holding people accountable is like nailing Jell-O to a wall. Decision-making was also a high-ranking item. When it is unclear who should be involved or what rights they have, decision-making is painfully slow. Power struggles, another frequently cited impediment, also regularly result from lack of role clarity, overlaid with a fair amount of ego. Lack of role clarity is

> Holding people accountable, decision-making and power struggles were all identified as top challenges. All can be traced back to issues of role clarity. ✓ **SURVEY**

at the root of the biggest challenges in the matrix and a major contributor to the ambiguity that afflicts matrix roles.

A university system client of mine was struggling to retain a high-level position. The turnover had been quick and public. It was a fact they shared almost as an aside. But the more we looked at their matrix capabilities, the more we realized the lack of role clarity at the top was not only causing redundant work, conflicting decisions and competition, it was causing turnover at the highest levels. They simply couldn't fill the spot (again) without figuring out a few kinks in their matrix. However, role clarity is also a bit of a red herring. It is an easy label to use when you don't want to say "I don't trust that person," "I don't like the way roles are defined" or "I don't like the power you hold over me." To get good at navigating this cross-functional challenge, you need to get to a true root cause.

Organizational charts, job titles and job descriptions are all great starting points for role clarity, but they certainly don't provide the full picture of a dynamic cross-functional role. Assumptions and misunderstandings happen in matrix roles because you are working without lane markers. As one interviewee described to me, "At the start of the year, the starting gun goes off, and you begin the race toward your goal. You may start in your own lane, but pretty soon everyone is focused on the finish line, not on their lane or who they are bumping into on their way down the track."

There will always be questions about "who does what" cross-functionally—there is no way to thoroughly and conclusively define roles in organizations as dynamic as these. A little investment in defining roles up front can provide a framework, and trust will help smooth out the rough edges. When the inevitable boundary breach comes up, dealing with it in the right way can not only resolve the conflict but strengthen the partnership.

Getting Things Right from the Start: Defining Roles

For key partners, decisions or tasks, an investment in deliberate role definition can make a huge difference in getting things done effectively and efficiently and building a partnership. Dae realized this as his relationship with Diana started to settle into the Dysfunctional Partner level.

The most widely used method for detailed role defining, called a RACI chart, outlines who is **R**esponsible, **A**ccountable, **C**onsulted or **I**nformed on a task or decision. RAPID (**R**esponsible, **A**ccountable, **P**erform, **I**nform, **D**ecide) and RASCI (**R**esponsible, **A**ccountable, **S**upporting, **C**onsulted, **I**nformed) are also variations.

For the Budget Planning Process, Dae and Diana's chart may have looked something like this:

DECISIONS/TASKS	RESPONSIBLE: Responsible for completing a work product	ACCOUNTABLE: Ensures this task is completed	CONSULT: Gives input into how task is carried out or into work product	INFORM: Kept apprised of progress and outcome
Working with cost center managers to complete budget paperwork	Dae	Bob (corporate process owner)	Angel	Diana
Producing budget planning reports	Dae	Bob (corporate process owner)	Diana	Angel
Planning agenda and logistics for budget review meeting	Diana	Rosa (Diana's boss)	Dae	Angel
Facilitating budget review meeting	Diana	Rosa (Diana's boss)	Dae	Bob (corporate process owner)
Finalizing budget reports	Dae	Bob (corporate process owner)	Diana	Angel
Sharing meeting output with cost center managers	Angel's management team	Angel	Dae	Diana

This approach steers you toward defining roles at ground level instead of at 30,000 feet. For Dae and Diana, the high-altitude distinction of "General Contractor" and "Specialist" wasn't enough. It wasn't until they talked about roles within a specific process (the budget planning process) and used a RACI tool that they reached a functional level of detail on their responsibilities.

The chart is a handy tool for moving quickly through action planning and decision-making. It can serve as an accountability mechanism and can be a safe starting place for conversations about role clarity. It positions the conversation as a discussion of what is happening vis-à-vis

"Perfect clarity would profit the intellect but damage the will."

BLAISE PASCAL

the outline, not your personal opinion. As one interviewee put it, "I use the RACI chart because when it comes to holding someone accountable for playing a specific role, the chart becomes the bad guy, not me."

The discussions that go into constructing a RACI-type chart are often as beneficial as the chart itself. They force a team or partnership to be very precise about the tasks and decisions in front of them and where and how they overlap and connect. This process promotes conversations that may not happen otherwise.

Because the dialogue that goes into creating the role document is so rich, bring as many people as is practical into this process. For a reporting relationship matrix, include both bosses and bring in the employee to review the document. For teams, bring the full team together to discuss and include their bosses in a review discussion. The closer people are to the construction of this plan and the more opportunity they have to ask questions, the better your product and their understanding will be.

Whether your role definition is high level or as detailed as a RACI chart, test for clarity and agreement by running it through some "what if" scenarios with your team or partner, or maybe even garner outside opinions. For example, Dae and Diana could have posed scenarios such as:

- What if one of us gets a question that is part of the other's role?

- Will a shift in timelines change the roles at all?

- How do we use each other's "input"? When do we need it, and when do we make the call ourselves?

> Bring as many people in on role clarity discussions as practical; being part of the process adds to understanding and ownership of the role definitions.
>
> **ZOOM OUT**

- What if we reach an impasse on a decision we need to make?

Whatever shape your role definition takes, make sure it is documented and accessible. Role clarity in matrix roles really never ends. It needs focus and consistent (if not constant) tending. Roles shift over time or reveal themselves differently based on the specific task or project, so updating this knowledge is key.

Three Simple Guidelines for Using Role Clarity Tools

Role clarity is a noble endeavor, but implemented incorrectly or for the wrong reasons, it can be damaging. This was painfully obvious for a client I worked with who had recently implemented a role definition guide for their product development teams. This story illustrates what can go wrong when you insert structured role clarity into an organization whose real issue is trust.

The organization was a US subsidiary of a large Japanese-owned company. They invested significant organizational resources on an initiative intended to clarify roles for roughly 10 different types of project team members using a RACI-type model. The final role document filled a two-inch binder. Six months after implementing this initiative, they asked me to conduct postmortem interviews with project team members to answer two questions: Were people using the role outline? Was the framework helping teams work more efficiently?

I interviewed project team members and learned that the binder *was* being used…as a weapon. The minute someone even looked like they might be stepping outside their role, another team member pounced, using the role document as support. When asked if it was used proactively in planning who would do what on a certain task, the response typically was, "No, more for lining up evidence of an infraction."

Marina was the vice president of one of the functions that was represented on the team, and she was especially critical of the role definitions. She told me about Seamus, a relatively new project manager who carried the binder around with him everywhere—passages highlighted, pages tabbed for easy reference. He was particularly keen on pointing out offenses committed by Marina's team, which made Marina and her team extremely defensive and mistrustful of him. This mistrust made them resist his efforts to enforce the guidelines of the document and sent them on a quest to identify *his* encroachments.

Seamus was the extreme, but not the exception. It became obvious through my conversations that many team members were gripping on to that role definition binder like it was their only floatation device in the middle of the ocean. For Seamus, and I suspect for others, this was killing his trustworthiness and credibility. In his singular focus on roles, he was losing sight of his own role—to make the project successful, specifically by bringing a new product to market.

It was also apparent that not only was the organization fixing the wrong problem, but their solution was actually making the real problem worse. Roles may not have been crystal clear, but the bigger issue was trust. Would teams that trusted each other need roles documented at this level of detail? Teams with high trust tend to move in and out of roles fluidly, not taking much offense if liberties are taken with how roles are carried out.

Finally, the teams were using the role definitions as a way to substantiate claims of boundary breach—basically using the tool against each other. These conflicts were divisive, not collaborative, and they were missing opportunities to use the role definition documents proactively in planning how they would get things done.

This story was about a large-scale organizational effort to clarify roles, but the same dynamics are involved in one-to-one situations (like Dae and Diana). Keep these three guidelines in mind on your quest for role clarity.

1. **Don't assume role clarity is the problem; look at trust.** Role clarity can seem like an easy solution for teams and partnerships—far easier than dealing with the fact that they don't trust each other. I have a former client (I was fired because of this specific point!) that considered RACI the "cornerstone of collaboration." RACI is not. Trust is. If someone is collaborating with you only because your name is in the right spot on the RACI, then you are in trouble and your collaboration will likely be short-lived. By itself, clarification of roles won't increase trust or improve a partnership or ensure sustained collaboration. But when coupled with genuine intent and actions to improve the partnership (like those outlined in Essential #1), role clarity can help put a relationship back on track, as in the case of Dae and Diana.

   > Your response should be based on the nature and impact of the boundary breach, your relationship with the person and the risk involved.
   >
   > **TRIAGE**

2. **Use role definitions offensively, not just defensively**. Any role clarity mechanism runs the risk of being used as a weapon. Especially in low-trust settings, it can become a conduit for trust issues. Role definitions are best used pro-actively, in initial project planning and as tasks or decisions emerge, not when you are reacting to a boundary breach and emotions are high. Boundary breaches are inevitable, but there are better ways to handle them (as described later in this chapter).

3. **Don't ever put it on the shelf.** Role clarity is a point in time, and the outline is a living document. There will be infractions. Sometimes those infractions can lead you to an even better, clearer definition. Revise and edit accordingly.

Dealing with Boundary Breach

Boundary breach will happen, no matter how thorough and inclusive your process or how comprehensive your outline. Although you don't want to carry your role binder around looking for a target, there will be times when you have to confront an infraction. But before you jump in, step back and ask three questions:

» Why did it happen?
» Is it worth confronting?
» What's the best way to confront it?

Why Boundary Breach Happens

A marketing team and a team of clinical experts (made up of physicians, nurses and pharmacists) were brought into a matrix to develop and commercialize complex products used in a hospital setting. Close collaboration between the marketing team and the clinical team was critical. The collaboration was not terribly effective, and, thinking that role clarity might be the cause, the team leaders asked me to help clarify the two teams' roles. After interviewing both teams, it was clear that there were a few people who were new on the team and simply not sure where their role stopped and another's started. But the more prevalent issue was that the clinical team didn't like taking orders from marketing, and marketing didn't like having to clear everything through clinical. Well-defined roles, just nobody liked them much.

Boundary breach happens for a variety of reasons ranging from innocently unaware to deliberately defying. The explanations can be thought of as a continuum:

Starting from the left side of the scale, "They didn't know" or "They forgot" is entirely plausible in a matrix. Chances are, the people in your web are also part of other webs, and unless your organization is really consistent about role definition, each of these has their own unique assumptions and guidelines around roles.

"They misunderstood" and "They thought it was an exception" are both evidence of the big gray area that remains even after you do a thorough job defining roles. Misunderstandings are bound to happen, because defining a role comprehensively and definitively is impossible. There will always be room for interpretation or wording that isn't entirely clear. As mentioned earlier, there is also a difference between the understanding of people who were "in the room" when the roles were defined and those handed the final product. The latter don't have the benefit of the discussion behind the paper, which will impact their understanding.

Exceptions crop up because there will be "what if" scenarios you didn't consider. Accounting for all possible exceptions is impossible. In addition, a matrix by definition is an amalgamation of many different perspectives and areas of expertise. What looks straightforward from one point of view (and therefore calling for the action as prescribed in your role definition) may look like an exception requiring a departure from the playbook from another person's point of view.

At the far-right side of the scale of explanations, we reach what I call *role acceptance*—the roles are clear, but we just don't like them. It is one thing to nod your head in acceptance to an outline of responsibilities on paper. But sometimes when those roles actually play out, acceptance is not so easy.

When to Tackle Role Conflicts

In a matrix role, you don't have the authority to force compliance; **JUJITSU** your approach will need to focus not only on resolution but building the partnership.

Assessing why the breach happened helps you assess the next step—choosing your course of action. Your response should be based on the nature and impact of the boundary breach, your relationship with the person and the risk involved.

Role clarity documents are great accountability mechanisms, but they aren't laws that need constant surveillance and enforcement. Show flexibility and trust by not addressing, discussing and debriefing every little infringement. This buys you wiggle room when you step out of your own agreed-upon role.

You should let it go if this is the first time you have seen the person make a particular mistake, and it doesn't have much of an impact on your goal or the morale of the people involved. Let it go if it is truly an exception that won't come up again. Also let it go if the politics created by addressing the issue are worse than the role infraction itself.

Tackling a conflict can take different forms (as discussed in the "Partnership-driven resolution" section)—ranging from a quick discussion focused on reminding them of the content of the role document to a conflict resolution discussion.

Here's when you want to approach people. In a clear case of misinformation or misunderstanding—don't miss the opportunity to refer them back to the role outline. When a trend becomes evident, with repeated infringements from the same person or on the same task, discuss it. If the behavior sets a precedent and permanently moves role markers, talk about it. And finally, you must confront if the behavior negatively impacts milestones, work product or team morale.

Partnership-Driven Resolution for Role Conflicts

When you have decided to tackle the boundary issue, a little planning is called for because the person you are approaching most likely is or should be a partner. Let's go back to the possible explanations for the boundary breach to determine your course of action:

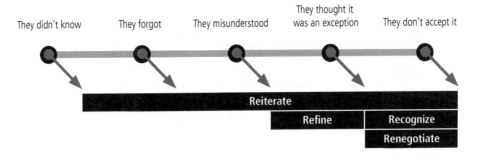

Not surprisingly, the explanations on the left side have one necessary action—reiterate the roles. A simple, "Hey by the way just wanted to remind/let you know" conversation is warranted.

As you move toward the middle, reiteration is still needed, but so is refining. Misunderstandings and exceptions should cause you to consider refining role definitions. "Hey by the way" might be followed with, "let's take a look at how we can tweak the role outline to make sure it is clearer and more useful for us."

In the case of lack of acceptance, or when there is a trend for repeated missteps by the same person, a number of carefully delivered messages are necessary. You will need to reiterate, potentially go as far as renegotiating roles and recognize that accepting the role may be difficult. Clearly, these are the trickiest circumstances. The first key is to walk in assuming it *is* one of the other circumstances. We tend to see our own boundary breaches as accidents or attempts to "help out," but see others as overstepping their bounds and encroaching on our territory. If you grant their intentions the same leniency that you grant you own, you will walk in assuming best intent—which sets the tone for the interaction.

> Do not assume they are rejecting the role as defined. Assume clarity is at issue.
>
> **MINDSET**

After a shift to "best intent" mindset, you will need to think about your message and your words. Here's how I might coach Dae and Diana, our Finance friends from earlier, on confronting each other on role acceptance.

	Say This ...	Not That ...
Start with a safe opening	"I wanted to circle back on the role agreements we set up last month…"	"I am here to talk to you about not following the commitments we laid out in the role document."
Keep it tentative and reiterate	"We had agreed that you would complete the paperwork and keep me informed, but I haven't heard anything from you on it. Maybe I missed an email from you?"	"Even though we agreed you would complete the paperwork and keep me informed, so far you have done nothing to keep me in the loop."
Recognize it may be tough to accept	"I know it must be frustrating having me in the middle of this with you and Angel, but I do think keeping me updated will help us better manage this consistently."	"You have to accept that I am involved in this, and it's not just you and Angel running this initiative."
Renegotiate	"Would it make more sense for us to just set up 30-minute calls each week, than to leave it impromptu?"	"You agreed to it, so you need to stick to it."

The difference between these two columns is significant. On the right you have a forceful and compliance-driven tone. The left is unassuming and aiming for agreement and ownership. In a matrix role, you don't have the authority to force compliance; your approach will need to focus not only on resolution but building the partnership.

These words may seem too soft for you, or not sound like you—that's OK. It isn't necessary to use them verbatim. You need to find your own style and way of positioning things. Just walking in assuming best intent, being tentative, asking questions and recognizing the difficulty of the situation will be huge trust builders.

The approach in this section assumes you have some sort of outline of roles. Agreed-upon role outlines are a powerful, objective starting point for these discussions. Without one, you have no basis for your claim, no point of reference, and you may even have to overcome judgments on why you are questioning their actions. Even if you don't do a full formal RACI chart, some sort of structured dialogue is vital to holding people accountable in matrix roles. It should outline roles around tasks and decisions and be documented and accessible.

Last Resort: Elevate It

Any role conflict has the potential to be sticky. Some are stickier than others. Although you don't want to overplay this card, there are times when you will need to pull in help to tackle a role issue. Issues involving acceptance can fall into this category. Acceptance often starts at the top. Remember the marketing and clinical teams that couldn't work together? Do you know who resisted those roles more than anyone? The leaders—there were disagreements on roles at the very top of the business unit, and they trickled down through the organization.

When the conflict is bigger than you—the infraction is a result of disconnects at a higher level—you will want to consider elevating it. If you have repeatedly approached the person on a role misstep and the behavior persists, you should elevate it. The same Rules of Elevation outlined in Essential #2 apply here.

When done well, bringing others in can be a powerful tool in resolving any type of conflict. Overplayed, it may send the wrong messages to your boss(es) and team. Use it sparingly and effectively on the trickiest of role conflicts.

> *"It takes generosity to discover the whole through others. If you realize you are only a violin, you can open yourself up to the world by playing your role in the concert."*
>
> JACQUES-YVES COUSTEAU

Sorting Out Solid and Dotted Line Responsibilities

One of the more frustrating role clarity issues is discerning the roles of the solid versus dotted line manager. Below you will see some generally accepted definitions, but more importantly when clarifying these roles, start with the business need behind the comanagement setup. Why is having two bosses necessary? What is it expected to accomplish? Too often we sprinkle these relationships around the organization with no rationale, no explanation to the employee or the managers on what this triad is intended to accomplish. Start with the why, then define the how. The why always informs the how. Here is an outline of how a typical dotted/solid line reporting relationship is defined:

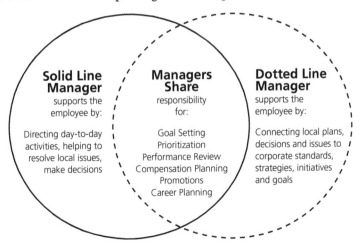

Solid Line Manager supports the employee by:

Directing day-to-day activities, helping to resolve local issues, make decisions

Managers Share responsibility for:

Goal Setting
Prioritization
Performance Review
Compensation Planning
Promotions
Career Planning

Dotted Line Manager supports the employee by:

Connecting local plans, decisions and issues to corporate standards, strategies, initiatives and goals

You'll never eliminate the ambiguity of matrix roles. There is a limit to how much a role can be defined, so you need to clarify what you can and get comfortable with the ambiguity that remains. Very few roles are unambiguous, and those that are would probably bore you to tears. Get used to it. Better yet, get good at it. Whether defining your role versus others in your web or keeping the roles of multiple bosses straight, role clarity is a journey, not a destination. Trying to completely eliminate ambiguity will just exhaust you and take your focus off your goals. The good news is that this ambiguity also holds the opportunity to shape your own role. If you embrace the freedom that ambiguity provides, you will find opportunities to try things outside of your box. Few people are motivated by ambiguity, but some are challenged by it and thrive in this type of environment. Be one of those people.

IN SUMMARY

EMBRACE

→ The fact that the nature of matrix roles means boundaries are blurred; get used to having your toes stepped on and stepping on others'

→ The need to be proactive in defining roles, but realistic in what role clarity can provide

→ Tackling the critical role conflicts in a partnership-driven way

WHERE TO START

→ Be as inclusive as possible when defining roles. If you are working with a team, consider bringing their direct bosses in as reviewers. Having them in the same room builds understanding and reinforces their role in making the person and the project successful

→ Use your role descriptors as tasks come up, not just on front-end planning. At the end of a meeting, run your team's to-do list through the role descriptors to make sure marching orders are clear. This reinforces the use of the tool and ensures consistency in how you label different roles.

→ Check in on role outlines—make changes, add details, ask others to review them.

→ Make sure role documents are user-friendly and accessible (on a shared drive, collaboration site, etc.)

→ When you are considering whether to confront a boundary breach, work through the situation with someone who isn't involved—they will be more objective about whether it is a breach big enough and important enough to confront.

IN PRACTICE

FOR LEADERS

If you comanage, make sure the roles are defined (and not just at a general level; sit down with your comanage partner and create definitions specific to your triad). Coach others on what to expect in terms of role overlap, ambiguity, etc. When people come to you with role clarity issues, get curious to determine if it is indeed a role clarity issue—make sure you are solving the right problem. When you enter into role clarity processes, like RACI, do so with the mindset of the benefit of the process over the product. Set expectations that the RACI must be supported by strong partnership and communication; in and of itself it will not eliminate ambiguity.

FOR CROSS-FUNCTIONAL/MATRIX TEAMS

Bring direct bosses into the team's role clarity discussions. Having them in the same room builds understanding and reinforces their role in making the person and the project successful. Role definitions and task assignments that are made in a team meeting may make perfect sense, but will they stand up to the test of the real world when bosses start to ask questions and influence what has been defined? Get them involved to pressure-test the role definition and get their buy-in.

WORKING VIRTUALLY

Understanding the roles of others in a virtual work environment is a bit like operating without one or more of your senses. You miss picking up on cues and information through osmosis like we do when we are colocated. You will have to be deliberate in understanding the roles of others. Ask questions, and if roles start feeling clunky, deal with it quickly—take overt action to clarify. And of course, put more emphasis on partnerships.

> *"It is not always what we know or analyzed before we make a decision that makes it a great decision. It is what we do after we make the decision to implement and execute it that makes it a good decision."*
>
> WILLIAM POLLARD

ESSENTIAL #4

GET DECISIONS MADE

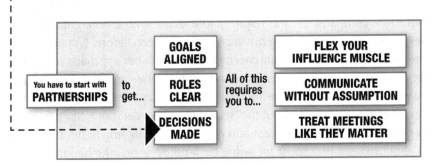

WHAT IT IS

Cross-functional decisions, like the matrix structure itself, bring together diverse perspectives, divergent agendas and priorities, and competing interests. Decisions tend to be complex, and there are high expectations for transparency and inclusion. You leverage partnerships, align goals and clarify roles. You bring to bear your influence, communication and meeting leadership skills.

WHAT THE RESEARCH SAYS

What's most important:
- » Making decisions in a timely manner

What's most likely to trip you up:
- » Making the decisions you should and knowing when to delegate to others on your team or others in the organization

Overall:
- » This is the most important thing for an organization to get right, with the highest likelihood of conferring a competitive advantage

VICTORIA

was a marketing manager in a recently acquired company. Seemingly overnight, she went from working in a small, founder-run business to being part of a multinational Fortune 500 entity. As a marketing manager (and really the only marketing person prior to acquisition), her decision-making rights and authority were crystal clear. But in the new company, she was required to straddle several different matrices, with levels of inclusion and consensus she had never seen before. Not unexpectedly, no one warned her of this or coached her on how her approach needed to change. She came in and did what she had always done—made decisions, told people what those decisions were and expected that they would carry things out. She started getting questions about the "why" behind her decisions. She perceived this as questioning of her judgment and responded by digging in her heels. She wasn't about to set a precedent for going back on decisions she had made. She was also questioned about "how" she made a decision, which completely confounded her—how did she make a decision? With her 15 years of working with this product from its inception, of course! How could one possibly break down into steps what just came naturally to her after seeing it all before?

The questions—while frustrating, annoying and just plain time-consuming—she could probably live with. What she couldn't live with was seeing that her decisions weren't being implemented. It was like people were ignoring her. Not only did they not follow her directives, they were downright resistant, and eventually a revolt began to brew. When given the feedback that she was running roughshod over people, failing to engage stakeholders and they weren't appreciating it, her response was, "I am just getting stuff done—it's like these people on our big, new 'mothership' are not interested in getting things done."

Key Differences between Decision-Making in Traditional and Matrix Roles

Victoria's scenario plays out in newly acquired companies all the time. I work with companies in this type of transition often, and it is so challenging to go from a streamlined, what I consider a more "traditional" way of making decisions to cross-functional decision-making. Even if you aren't making a transition like Victoria, cross-functional decision-making may run counter to your natural "I know my stuff, I'm ready...DECIDE!" mindset.

Decision-making in a traditional role is like running a quarter-mile race around a track—clear start and finish, clear lanes. Cross-functional decision-making is an obstacle course. It requires you to sprint, slow down, jump, crawl, zig and zag. If you go into a cross-functional decision thinking and running like it is a race around a track, you will frustrate yourself and those around you and most likely not reach the finish line.

Over 70% of the people surveyed for this book listed getting decisions made, figuring out who **SURVEY** the decision maker is and including the right people as top challenges in matrix roles.

Victoria was the star of the quarter-mile sprint in her role prior to the acquisition. But because no one told her that the track was now an obstacle course, she continued to sprint, plowing right through the obstacles. There are definitely times when plowing down is called for—but it's probably not when you join a new team, and it can't serve as your primary strategy in a matrix role. For Victoria, employing this strategy early and often was resulting in diminishing returns. Here are a few of the key distinctions she and others miss:

	Decisions in your "Lane"	Decisions in a Traffic Circle
Making the Decision	• Hierarchy/title-driven • Straightforward, linear • Often behind closed doors, unstructured • Often exclusive	• Expertise, role, input-driven • Complex, much back and forth • Need for transparent process • Inclusive
Executing the Decision	• Authority-driven • Communication on the "what" of the decision • Requires little follow-up	• Ownership-driven • Communication is transparent on the what, why, how and who • Can require significant follow-up
Key Challenges	Making the right decision and using authority to implement	• Balancing decision-making speed with inclusion • Knowing who is the ultimate decision-maker • Gaining ownership in the decision to make it "stick"

Five Rules for Getting Decisions Made in a Matrix Role

As one of my interviewees put it, "decision-making in a matrix is less about 'making' and more about 'finessing.'" This "finessing" requires adherence to five rules:

» Rule #1: Balance and toggle your decision-making styles
» Rule #2: Watch your biases
» Rule #3: Set it up right
» Rule #4: Invest in agreement
» Rule #5: Go the extra mile to make sure the decision sticks

Decision-making in a matrix requires more give and take, more finesse than force.

JUJITSU

Rule #1: Balance and Toggle Your Decision-Making Styles

The bane of Victoria's existence in her new role was the seemingly endless number of people who had input, interest or pure curiosity into her decisions and decision-making process. She did what many people in matrix roles do—she reacted to others' need for inclusion and information by drawing more distinct lines in her sandbox. She let fewer and fewer people in and became less forthcoming about her decisions and decision-making process. What she may have gained in the speed of decision-making, she was losing on the implementation end because of the lack of ownership that exclusive decision-making can create.

For people like Victoria who are used to calling the shots, the inclusion-based nature of matrix decision-making is the biggest and most critical adjustment you must make to be successful. Even when a decision appears to be yours and yours alone, chances are the decision will be better if you get input from others, and chances are you will need others to make your decision happen. Simply put: input in making the decision makes the decision better and builds ownership in the implementation. Both of these are critical given how interwoven most decisions are and how much you will need to rely on influence versus authority to make decisions happen.

Even when a decision appears to be yours and yours alone, chances are the decision will be better if you get input from others, and chances are you will need others to make your decision stick.

MINDSET

Victoria represents one end of the spectrum. Now meet Marcus—Victoria's polar opposite. Marcus was a quality manager for a manufacturing company, with a dual-reporting relationship with the head of Quality and the plant manager at his site. He included everyone on everything. Even for the smallest decisions, he brought in both bosses. He didn't want to discount one or the other, he wanted to make sure all three of them were in agreement. At his year-end performance review, the bosses raised the white flag. They could no longer take the overinclusion and the time it was consuming. "Just do it!" they implored.

The consensus Marcus sought wasn't ill intended, just ill placed. Consensus (seeking the best possible decision that all stakeholders can live with) is an important strategy in cross-functional decision-making. But it is overused, and because it is overused, it gets a bad rap. We tend to swing from being self-appointed sheriffs (Victoria) to camp counselors trying to get everyone to agree and hold hands for every decision (Marcus). Good matrix managers balance the need for speed with the need for inclusion and by doing this, toggle between various decision-making styles.

There are several options for your matrix decision-making approach. But in a matrix role, a couple of things are not options. The first is getting input. Given the complex interwoven nature of the problems and solutions, input is required in nearly every cross-functional decision. Broad-based involvement in implementation is also not optional—many decisions will be bigger than your area of responsibility, and you will have to reach out to give a decision arms and legs. But what lies in

For input and implementation of decisions, you must look broadly at who to bring in.

ZOOM OUT

the middle is where you can (and must) expand and contract—it's how the decision is actually made. Most effective matrix decision-making processes look something like this:

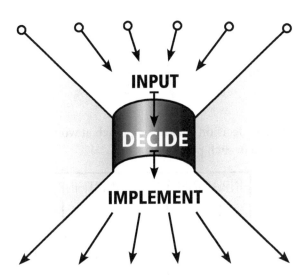

The center of this flow of input and implementation—the actual activity of deciding—can and should grow and shrink based on the decision. Even graphically it is balanced and stable. Compare this to what Victoria's approach might look like in visual form:

89

DECIDE

IMPLEMENT

For her, not only did the center shrink, so did the top and bottom of the funnel, leaving her with a decision with very little stability and staying power. This approach works fine with a decision that only affects you and only requires you to implement—but those are rare in a cross-functional role. Even if Victoria didn't bring others in on the decision-making, she would have been better served by investing in a broader reach for implementation to give things a bit of stability:

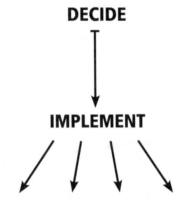

DECIDE

IMPLEMENT

If we drew Marcus' decision-making approach, it would resemble a square—he involved everyone in each phase:

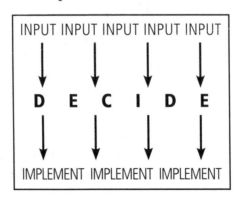

Although the visual makes it appear balanced and stable, the investment is just not worth it. It's like taking apart the engine of a car to change the oil. The investment is neither practical nor necessary.

Matrix mastery requires you to toggle between different decision-making strategies—to grow and shrink that center portion as it fits the decision and to provide reinforcement by bringing others into the process. It also means knowing when your decision-making approach isn't working and you need a Plan B. For example, if you are going for group consensus and get stuck, you should move to a single decision maker—more on that later in the chapter.

If you are like Marcus, the narrowing point of matrix decision-making often proves troublesome, because it ruffles feathers. No one wants to make the call on who's in and who's out. Alternatively, if roles aren't clear, we truly can't put our finger on who the decision maker is or who should be included. Both scenarios lead to the same result: we let everyone in on the decision, and decision-making grinds to a halt.

Knowing whom to pull in when is the key to balancing inclusion with speed and toggling between different decision-making approaches. You have to narrow at some point. Having clear roles helps (Essential #3), as do these considerations:

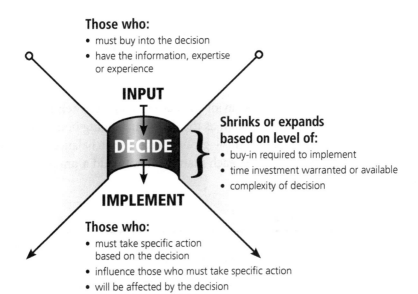

Those who:
- must buy into the decision
- have the information, expertise or experience

INPUT

DECIDE

Shrinks or expands based on level of:
- buy-in required to implement
- time investment warranted or available
- complexity of decision

IMPLEMENT

Those who:
- must take specific action based on the decision
- influence those who must take specific action
- will be affected by the decision

At each step, transparency is key. People need to know why you are including them or not including them. Be up front about this process (giving input is different from being part of the decision-making group). There will always be people who want to be included but aren't. Be forthcoming with this as well.

Rule #2: Watch Your Biases

The human brain is wired for bias. We aren't robots and we don't work on algorithms; we think and decide based on shortcuts. And the dicier things get, the more the bias comes into play (we've seen every bias under the sun during the pandemic as we tried to process all the information coming at us). Here are a few better-known biases:

- The **Recency Effect** says we tend to place more importance on information or events that we experience most recently.

- The **Primacy Effect** occurs when we put more weight on events or information we hear first.

- If we are subject to **Confirmation Bias**, we search for or interpret information that confirms our opinion.

- With **Distinction Bias**, we may view two options as more dissimilar when evaluating them simultaneously than when evaluating them separately.

- If you read this and think you don't have biases, or at least not as many as others do, then you just fell into the **Bias Blind Spot**—the tendency to see oneself as less biased than other people.

Biases are natural to human behavior and can't be completely eliminated. The fact that groups function more often as the decision-making bodies in matrix organizations helps allay some of this—group members can balance each other's biases or call them out. However, each matrix role can add a unique set of biases to beware of:

Matrix Role	Matrix Bias
Reporting Relationship	Align more closely with one boss versus another based on common function, geography, exposure or style.
Customer Hub	Align so vehemently with a customer that it impacts ability to understand and appreciate the perspective/needs of the internal matrix
Project Team	Align so vehemently with a project that it impacts ability to understand and appreciate the perspective/needs of the functions represented on the team
Cross-Functional Team	Put more weight on information from your own functional area because of your understanding and familiarity with it

You need to be doubly diligent in watching for bias in matrix decision-making. Not only must you watch for common decision biases but matrix-specific biases. Bias can hamper your ability to get the right people involved, get the full picture of the considerations and implications of a decision and implement fully and effectively.

Rule #3: Set It Up Right

A route that you have driven many times becomes rote, subconscious, automatic. Drive the same route with someone following you who has never driven it before, and your approach will be very different. You lay out your route with them prior to leaving, slow down, check your mirror and put your blinker on earlier. You invest more effort both before and during your journey to get you both there safely.

Cross-functional decision-making is a bit like that. It is very conscious, very structured and planned out—there must be up-front investment. You need to plan things out and check in frequently to make sure everyone is still with you. When you are taking others along for the ride, there has to be a well-defined process that starts at the moment you realize a decision needs to be made and continues until the decision is thoroughly implemented or embedded in the organization.

Here are the general elements for setting up a decision:

Name it: It sounds simple, but a good decision-making process starts by recognizing that there is a decision on the table and labeling it. "OK, we have a decision here—do we want to limit the review period to two days or extend to four?" Calling this out defines the start of the process and is also a great way to check that everyone agrees that this is indeed the decision on the table. For instance, in this example, the decision very well could be whether there should be a limit on review time at all. A subtle difference, but the frame shifts how you will make the decision. When I ask leaders or leadership teams to describe decisions they have made in the past month, I am generally met with blank stares. Teams struggle to articulate decisions, and leaders are caught flat-footed. The optimist in me wants to believe decision-making is such a natural part of what they do that describing it is like asking someone to describe that last breath they took. The realist in me believes we do a lousy job labeling decisions and initiating the decision-making process. Why is this important in cross-functional roles? Because you are bringing others with you along the way—to get input, define options, make the decision, communicate the decision and execute the decision. You can't do any of that unless you say, "This is the decision we have to make." You must lay it on the table.

Label it: Remember our discussion earlier in the chapter about Victoria and Marcus' decision-making approaches and the options you have? It can be group input with a singular decision maker, consensus or consensus with a fallback (work toward consensus for a defined period of time and if consensus is not reached, it defaults to a decision by a specific, named person). Let people know which it is. Nothing is more frustrating than thinking you are part of the decision-making process only to find that you have input but aren't a decision maker. Remember, people tend to have high inclusion needs and assumptions in matrix roles. If and how you are including them needs to be transparent so that they understand what is expected of them and can participate appropriately.

Identify the decision-maker...or don't: I have clients who spend months outlining decision-making rights because we assume it's always easier when you know who that one person is who will make the call. Outlining decision-making rights is great if you can anticipate all possible decisions/decision categories. But the industries I work with are about as complex as they get, and rote, repeatable decisions just aren't the norm. As a university-based colleague said to me, "Susan, our university is focused on solving society's more complex problems...who knows what those will be and the decisions that will be required."

Don't get me wrong, outlining decision-making rights, just like RACIs, is not a bad thing to do. It just doesn't solve all your problems. I would love for organizations to clarify where they can around decision-making rights, but then outline this: *What does a team do when a decision-maker isn't obvious?* Is it expected that they stop until they get that figured out, or just keep deciding? Does it default to the highest-ranking person in the group? Go straight to the top of the organization? That's where the gold is, knowing that will help teams navigate this much faster.

One of the things that I have found effective is reframing it to, "Who's our tie-breaker?" "Tie-breaker" is just for this one decision, just to keep things moving, not a declaration of power or a precedent that is set. Teams can usually identify a tie-breaker more readily than a decision-maker. Maybe it's just semantics, but it tends to help things move along when a team gets stuck.

Set the criteria: Without criteria, decision-making can go on endlessly—especially in a matrix, where individual criteria can usurp collective criteria and get in the way of the ever-present trade-offs required. Set the criteria (again, the more inclusive, the better) and keep them front and center for all those involved in decision-making. The criteria you use will also facilitate implementation—people are more likely to accept a decision that went through a vigorous criteria-based process. And they will always want to know the "why" behind a decision. These natural tendencies are even stronger in a matrix organization because those on the receiving end are being asked to do something, stop doing something or change the way they are doing something by someone who most likely doesn't have direct authority over them.

Because cross-functional decisions attempt to bring together multiple diverse perspectives, personalities and needs, they require diligent setup. While the setup may seem like it is taking up time, the investment in time helps you pick up speed in reaching agreement by getting everyone working on the same page. It saves time in implementation, as you will get fewer questions when those implementing understand and respect the process that was followed. Not to mention, your decision quality can be improved by employing an objective, methodical process. Remember the four key mindsets outline in the intro chapter? One of them was be cautious of those things that feel fast but actually slow you down. This is a great example of how slowing down can actually help you pick up speed.

For cross-functional decision-making, go slow to go fast.

MINDSET

Rule #4: Invest in Agreement

I was working with a company on an initiative to change their culture. They had outlined a number of key behaviors they wanted instilled into the culture, including two that were critical: supporting team decisions in word and deed, and open debate. At first we struggled because these behaviors seemed to be in opposition—one was supportive and the other required questioning and challenging. But the more we talked, the more we realized that supporting team decisions was entirely dependent on the opportunity to debate them. People found it difficult to support team decisions if they weren't engaged in debate at some point in the process, and their commitments carried less weight without debate. What's more, after discussing this, we also realized another piece of the company culture—continually "remaking" decisions—was caused by the same issue. Decisions were reopened because people either weren't engaged or didn't feel heard in the initial decision-making phase. The organization wasn't investing in agreement, and they were paying a price in implementation as well as in the quality of the decision.

If you have ever observed a team reaching agreement, you know how unsightly it can be. The process can be difficult. Behind every well thought-out, effectively implemented decision is a progression of back and forth and up and down that shouldn't be short-circuited. My writing coach, Wally Bock, explained the difference between a good chapter and a great chapter by comparing it to microwaved food and conventionally cooked food—"Microwaved food doesn't taste as good because it didn't go through the process." The same can be said of decisions. Reaching agreement isn't about shortcutting the process—we can't microwave it. At the same time, you can't stay in the process forever—to continue the cooking analogy, you don't want to boil everything down to mush. It's about making investments in the process to make it more focused and efficient.

Decision-making starts by following Rules 1–3. It should involve a handful of key decision makers who are deputized to make the decision—not stand-ins, not representatives, but real decision makers—unfettered by bias and working on a clearly laid out decision, process and criteria.

After that, the dialogue kicks in, your investment in agreement begins, and your role as facilitator is in high gear. As I coach teams I often remind them, talking is not deciding. You can't chat your way to consensus. It needs to be a structured dialogue. Here are a few keys to going through the process but not getting mired in it.

Use meetings: A well-run meeting (as described in Essential #7) is to decision-making what a great set of tires is to a race car. Meetings give you speed, traction and stability when you are seeking to reach agreement. To do it well, you must think through the sequence of review, analysis and discussion that is necessary to reach concurrence. Once you lay that out, determine at which points a meeting is necessary. From there follow the steps here as well as in Essential #7.

Use white space: How you use the time before and between meetings is as important as the meetings themselves. White space is a dangerous place in matrix organizations. This is where decisions get forgotten, decision makers become distracted and your whole process can fall apart. During this time, work one on one with decision makers, follow up on questions and ensure they are doing their homework. Don't let the pending decision get lost in the throng of other matrix priorities.

Set a time limit and have a Plan B: Whether it is one hour or one year, set a time limit for reaching agreement and let them know what happens after you reach that limit. Does it become majority vote? Does the decision get elevated to a higher-level decision maker? Do you make it? Someone else? A large-scale project leader I spoke with told me he initiated decision-making with teams with this preamble: "You can either make the decision in the next…[whatever timeframe]…or I will make it. And I assure you, I will be totally unencumbered by fact." The thought of someone else making the decision for them is usually a great motivation to work hard toward agreement.

Pull back to look at the overall objective: It is easy for people to slip back into representing only their piece of the matrix in the heat of decision-making. Periodically pull back and remind them of the bigger-picture objective. Amir, a former GM of a large business, told this wonderful story about a decision he was making with one of his matrix partners. An issue arose with a product that fell into both business units: there was a decision of which business would get the gross profit. Prior to the meeting, Amir and his team pulled together all of the facts that would support his division getting the gross profit. It is probably safe to assume his partner did the same. Things got heated in the meeting as both sides made their case. Finally Amir said, "This is crazy. There's only one stock price. You can take 100%. If it doesn't affect the stock price, it doesn't matter who gets it." A decision that had been argued for three months was resolved in five minutes, and Amir and his team became known as the reasonable team players.

Periodically pull back and remind people of the bigger-picture objective **ZOOM OUT** to ensure they don't fall back into their side of the matrix in the heat of decision-making.

Sometimes giving or giving in sets the stage for influencing decisions **JUJITSU** later on.

Take a vote and ask what it would take: When you are in the middle of decision-making, occasionally go back to your criteria and, if there are options on the table, take a quick vote to see how far apart you are. Ask those in the minority what it would take to push them to another option. Most likely, you will come up with a new set of alternatives and be closer to agreement.

Use scenarios: Sometimes taking things out of the hypothetical can present new options or be the tipping point for agreement. When you are getting close to a decision, play the options out. Given the complexity of cross-functional decisions, you may be creating unintended consequences, and this may lead you to different options or closer to consensus. Scenarios are also helpful in checking agreement. If you have landed on a consensus decision: "We are going to extend the review period to two weeks," check agreement by asking scenario questions: "So that means that even when we have a priority project, we are going to allow the committee two weeks to review?" Simple questions like this can ensure that your agreement is solid.

Facilitating these decision-making discussions is challenging—people do this for a living. Acting as the facilitator can be tough when most likely you are also one of the decision makers and/or implementers of the decision. If it is a critical decision with sticky political angles, consider bringing in a third party. That will lend objectivity to the process and allow you to participate in the discussion.

Rule #5: Go the Extra Mile to Make Sure the Decision Sticks

Most of the companies I work for make good decisions; where they fall short is on implementation. The only thing tougher than getting a cross-functional decision made is getting it to stick across functions, geographies and levels. Lack of adhesion is often a symptom of the process, not the decision itself. There are three components that help ensure a decision sticks: (1) a structured, credible decision-making process, (2) including the right people in the right way and (3) consistent, transparent communication and follow-up. Often times we are so fatigued by the decision or distracted by the next one that we don't do justice to this important step. Here's what can happen when you are missing a piece:

A structured, credible process	Include the right people in the right way	Consistent, transparent communication and follow-up	Your decision is likely to be:
X	X	X	Implemented and integrated
	X	X	Questioned
X		X	Overturned or ignored
X	X		Forgotten or splintered

Even if you make the right up-front investments in terms of designing and executing a strong process and involving the right people, sometimes you get tired or have moved on to the next issue come implementation time. As a result, implementation is abandoned or approached halfheartedly. Implementation has to be a formal step in the process, and all parties must appreciate that their work isn't done once the decision is made. You must be as disciplined in communicating out and driving implementation as you are in making the decision. The members of the decision-making group must be united and see themselves as "decision shepherds." They are responsible to navigating the decision through the organization, skeptics and push back.

Consistent, transparent communication and follow-up requires answering the following questions:

- Who will be impacted or need to implement the decision? Who influences those who are impacted or will be called on to implement it?

- What do they need to know about the decision, why it was made and how it was made?

- What do they need to know or be able to do to implement it?

- What will be barriers to them implementing?

- How can you overcome these barriers through follow-up and communication with them?

What's at Risk: Decision Splintering

There is a reality and a risk in poor decision implementation. We fall prey to the aforementioned decision fatigue or lose focus, and hard-earned, well-thought-out decisions just disappear, or worse—they splinter.

What do I mean by splinter? This is a classic cross-functional scenario. The decision-making group decides on (let's keep this simple) switching from brown to blue conference room chairs. The blue is part of the company's branding and visual remake to attract talent in their hyper-competitive industry. It was a long, drawn-out, contentious decision, and they are exhausted, so their decision-making implementation amounts to an email. This email is picked up by Monique, whose team picked out the brown chairs (and we all know owners of the current state are prone to be your biggest haters) and who are responsible for the physical exchange of hundreds of chairs. So first, the group made a mistake in not including Monique, but then they doubled down with this implementation-by-email approach. Monique is already having a bad day when she gets the email.

She goes immediately to her team with comments like, "You are not going to believe what they did now...I know, I know but no one asked me...this is just another example of lack of respect from them." And the we/they narrative is built. More decisions like this fortify the narrative and splinters a cross-functional organization. This is how cross-functional organizations fall apart and push people back into their siloes. Decision implementation is key. Pushing the fatigue away, staying focused, responding to the questions posed above and seeking out the Moniques in your organization for special white-glove treatment not only increases the likelihood of your decision sticking, it increases the health of the cross-functional enterprise.

A Final Word: Winners and Losers

When I share this mindset with clients, they often visibly cringe. I work with really nice clients and I am grateful that this kind of tough talk makes them cringe and gets their attention. When we get to this point in our chat, I say, "In cross-functional decision-making, there are always winners and there are always losers, and you need to start recognizing that and calling it out—it's the elephant in the room that everyone needs to make friends with." What do I mean by this? In any truly cross-functional decision, you have competing needs and preferences. Not everyone's needs and preferences can be met (and if you make a decision that fulfills the needs and preferences of everyone in the organization, then your customers or shareholders or board of directors or someone in your orbit is going to pay). So why not just say it? Maybe "winners and losers" is harsh, but it's clear. Let's go back to the traffic circle. Do you know how they measure traffic circles? Throughput—how many cars they can get through. They don't measure how fast an individual car gets through—they don't care. It's all about overall throughput. Cross-functional decisions are like that. A decision's "goodness" is not measured by the impact on one team, location or function. It's measured at a higher level. When implementing and communicating decisions, people need to know this. And they need leaders who are honest with them.

So if I was coaching Monique, here's what I'd recommend she say: "Guys, this is a tough decision for us, and it will mean more work for us. But at a company level, people are really focused on bringing more employees in; you know we are all so un-

In decision-making in the matrix, you often need to go slow to go fast.

MINDSET

derstaffed right now. This is just one part of an overall plan to help us look the part of the coolest employer in the industry. So yes, you could consider it a loss for us because of the extra effort, but it's a win for us all if we can start bringing more talent in and lighten our load."

But Monique can only do that if the cross-functional decision-making team members act as shepherds and thoroughly communicate the what, why and how to her, and the organizational culture expects Monique to do the same.

Following these five rules takes time but helps you pick up speed in the long term. Adjust your expectations and approach with this in mind. As a 25-year veteran of several large matrix organizations told me, "What I found, and I still find it, is that we view the process and the conversations that are part of getting cross-functional decisions made as a either a luxury or a speed bump. They are neither, and once we wrap our heads around this, we can get better at decisions and get better decisions." What will also help is our next Essential, Flex Your Influence Muscle. Whether you are trying to reach a decision or affect how people implement it, influence is required.

IN SUMMARY

EMBRACE

→ Inclusion balanced with speed is the name of the game in matrix decision-making

→ Good decisions require investments on the back end in terms of thinking through the process and on the front end to ensure implementation.

→ Gaining agreement is an investment, not only in the decision, but in the implementation of that decision.

→ Decision implementation in a matrix will take as much focused, concerted effort as the making of the decision.

WHERE TO START

→ Review your recent decisions. Were you broad enough in your input? Were you able to narrow who you included on making the decision?

→ To watch for bias, assign a watch dog on your team or a colleague (to watch you specifically). Ask this person to raise a flag when they see a bias playing into decision-making.

→ When you are making a decision as a team, keep the decision, the criteria and the bigger-picture goal visible—literally. If you are in a room together, have it on flipcharts. If working asynchronously, have it at the top of a page or beginning of a document that they are reviewing.

→ Review the implementation of your recent decisions. Are there certain people or parts of your matrix that you are neglecting in terms of communication and follow-up? What is that costing you?

IN PRACTICE

FOR LEADERS

Cross-functional decisions tend to be complex, and there are high expectations for transparency and inclusion. How leaders make and implement decisions and the decisions they choose to take on (versus delegate) can't help but impact the "what" and "how" of decisions throughout the organization. In decision-making, like so many aspects of life, we tend to give what we get. If we are on the receiving end of decisions that are made exclusively, made at the wrong level or implemented poorly, we will do the same. Your decision-making behaviors (more so than your expressed expectations) will drive the decision-making of those in your organization. As mentioned before, watch for elevation—don't be tempted to take on every decision that makes its way down to you. In addition, don't pull decisions up to your level—the power of a matrix organization lies in dispersed decision-making, decision-making at the closest point of the problem. When leaders swoop in, you create a unwielding hybrid of decentralized and hierarchy-based decision-making that is frustrating, time-consuming and disempowering.

FOR CROSS-FUNCTIONAL/MATRIX TEAMS

Investing in agreement is critical here, as most of the decisions will be made as a team. Have a well laid-out, replicable process for making decisions. Set parameters for how long you will strive for consensus and what happens when you can't reach consensus. Also, make very sure that the people on your teams are "deputized." Make sure they can make decisions for the functions they represent. If they are unable to make decisions and have to continually go back to their function for validation, you have the wrong person on the team or their functional boss/team is not clear on what their role is on your team.

WORKING VIRTUALLY

Decision-making will take more time when it's virtual—assume that and build that into any plans you have. Break decision-making down into smaller virtual chunks and manage the "white space" between these conversations by thoroughly documenting progress at each step and checking in with people between conversations. Decisions will need even more structure and outline steps for the process. Visuals will be critical—I find when my clients are working virtually, there is no meeting that doesn't have slides. The visual helps keep us focused when we are not in the room together.

"You cannot antagonize and influence at the same time."

JOHN KNOX

ESSENTIAL #5
FLEX YOUR INFLUENCE MUSCLE

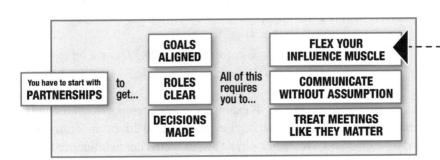

WHAT IT IS

In matrix roles, your accountabilities and responsibilities always exceed your formal power. Lacking in power, influence is all you've got.

WHAT THE RESEARCH SAYS

What's most important:
- » Being clear and succinct in expressing your ideas

What's most likely to trip you up:
- » Influencing through others (engaging stakeholders to influence other stakeholders).

SIMONE was a physician in a leadership role for a hospital system change-out. With a solid line to the Chief Medical Officer and a dotted line to the Chief Information Officer, she was dead center at the intersection between the standardization aims of the IT department and the innovation ambitions of the clinicians at the hospital. This quote from my interview with her was striking:

> *"It's frustrating to go to work, engage in something I have a lot of passion and pride in and yet have so few victories."*

She went on to share a series of examples of her attempts to get traction and influence on both sides of her matrix. IT expected her to drive standardization and get everyone on board. Her fellow physicians expected her to influence IT so that they could "have it their way" in terms of system configuration. She said, "Every time I gain traction with the clinical side, IT says I am going rogue. Every time I gain traction on standardization, I am a hero in IT and the goat to physicians."

Added to this was the fact that the two sides also had very different expectations of the style and method of influence she would employ. Her dotted line boss in IT told her, "Go out and kick their asses into line." Her solid line boss on the clinical side implored her to "be nice and work with them."

Even the partnerships with the two bosses were polar opposites. Her solid line was a long-time trusted colleague; her dotted line a new leader in the hospital with whom she had little history, and what history there was wasn't terribly pleasant. How did she influence?

> *"Small, short-term achievements that I set for myself keep me going—I see a lot that needs to be done but can't influence it all, so I stay focused. I also remind myself and anyone I come in contact with what the bigger picture is. It's not about what one side of the house or another thinks is right; it is about the path that we all eventually meet up with at the organizational level. And it's not about winning every battle with both sides of my matrix or pleasing both—that's impossible."*

Her biggest mistake?

> *"Being too unwavering at the beginning. I wasn't willing to give or let them sway me. This only got them defensive and created barriers that I am breaking down now to influence them."*

Building Influence Muscle in Matrix Roles

Simone's concentration on influence is warranted. In conducting the research for this book, influence was second only to building relationships and trust as the most important matrix skill identified—all of which play off each other in the way you get things done. This is because crisscrossing lines of authority and accountability leave matrix roles without much formal, sanctioned power. Fortunately, influence isn't something you have or you don't: it is a muscle you develop.

Stephen Covey begins *The 7 Habits of Highly Effective People* with the concept of Circle of Influence/Circle of Concern. Here's my interpretation of it and how it applies to influence in cross-functional roles.

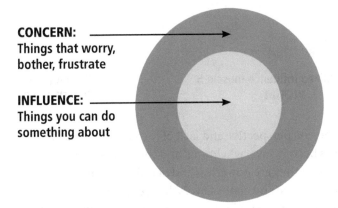

In Covey's description, among the concerns that enter your consciousness, there are some you can do something about and others you can't. His advice is to focus on those you can influence and let the others go—don't let them take up your time or energy. This is exactly what Simone does in setting her own "small short-term achievements." She stays focused on where she can influence.

Opportunities to influence abound in cross-functional roles—I realized this as I listened to Simone describe her situation. From her purview, she sees more than most people, which is not unique. Simone is not alone. When I ask workshop participants what percentage of their jobs they get done through their formal authority and not through influence, their average answer is 11%.

Matrix roles are usually built around critical initiatives (in the case of project teams or cross-functional teams), critical junctions (in the case of dual-reporting relationships) or critical customers (in the case of a customer hub). Sitting at an intersection provides you with a unique vantage point—you see things that others haven't noticed yet. You see holes, issues, decisions that need to be made, conversations that need to take place. In Covey's terms, more enters your Circle of Concern.

All those extra data and observations entering your Circle of Concern can do funny things to your influence muscle. You can easily fall into one of two traps:

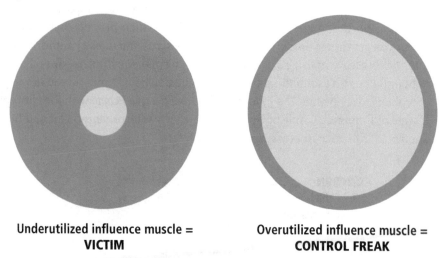

Underutilized influence muscle =
VICTIM   Overutilized influence muscle =
CONTROL FREAK

For some, the perspective and lack of formal power that are characteristic of matrix roles become overwhelming, and they go into victim mode, convincing themselves that they are powerless and blaming the matrix for everything. Others attempt to corral and control everything to gain comfort in the matrix, which is exhausting, dilutive and builds up resentment from the stakeholders around them. By overusing their influence they become like that billboard you see every morning on your way to work—at first it gets everyone's attention, but eventually it just blends in with the scenery.

Deciding to Wield Your Influence Muscle

Simone, our subject from the opening story, was very judicious in wielding her influence. As a matter of fact, this is one of the things that kept her sane in her influence-rich role.

You should clearly act on issues that are within your sphere of influence and have a high impact on your team and/or project. By the same token, those issues that are not within your influence and have a low impact should be left by the wayside. But there are plenty of variations in between. Here is a way to think about triaging items that enter your Circle of Concern:

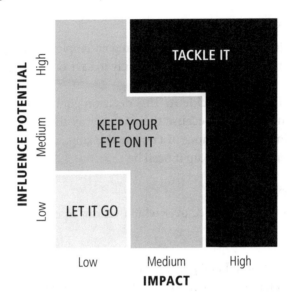

The idea here is that you have a range of options—from completely letting go to charging ahead at full throttle. Understanding this range helps you keep a balance. When you are triaging, be sure to challenge your historic boundaries. In a situation where your automatic assumption is that you can't influence, think again about what you could possibly do. If the issue is something that histori- cally you have tackled but with mixed results, skip it and see how the situation plays out without your influence (sometimes the most influential thing you can do is to choose not to influence). Also, watch for items to shift either in impact or your influence level and readjust accordingly.

Jean-Luc is a director of Materials for a US-based manufacturing company. His story provides a good example of this type of balance. His daily triage of influence opportunities is driven by his solid line reporting relationship to his country manager in France and dotted line reporting relationship to the head of Global Supply Chain in the US. Here are three items that recently came across his desk:

OPPORTUNITY #1
The Global Supply Chain function has scheduled a weeklong leadership summit

in the US in July (four months from now). The session conflicts with the vacation schedules of every member of his team.

Jean-Luc's Decision: Keep an eye on it. These training times tend to shift, so he will give it one month and see if he then has to influence the timing.

OPPORTUNITY #2

The global project team he is on is designing an employee engagement survey, and they want to distribute it in English only to save on expenses.

Jean-Luc's Decision: Tackle it. This decision could completely derail the results for his location because there is no way they will get accurate responses to in-depth questions in a non-native language. He has a voice on the team and can call for backup if need be.

OPPORTUNITY #3

Jean-Luc's two bosses disagree over which vendor to choose for an important raw material.

Jean-Luc's Decision: Let it go. There is not much he can do to influence either one of them on this issue. Realistically, the difference between the two vendors from his team's perspective is minimal.

Again, with so much coming at you that needs attention and influence, you have got to become good at distinguishing those that you need to invest time and energy and exert muscle on and those that have low return or little chance of traction.

Influence Ingredients: Proactive and In the Moment

There are two types of people who can influence—those who are persuasive conversationalists and those who build up influence equity over time. Not surprisingly, the latter are the ones who can have sustained influence in the matrix.

In cross-functional positions you are either influencing a current partner (and through this influence opportunity have a chance to develop the partnership to the next level or leverage the current state of the partnership) or you are influencing someone who may well be a partner in the future. Influence in matrix roles rarely happens in isolation—it usually isn't the first or last interaction with the person you are trying to influence. What that means is that your level of influence starts well before you jot a few persuasive ideas down on paper or put together a couple of compelling PowerPoint slides. It also means that how you handle the opportunity to influence impacts not only the issue at hand but also your partnership and future influence prospects.

There are six critical ingredients specific to influence in matrix roles that come into play. Three happen prior to influence; the other three in the moment of influencing. Here's what they are and how they play out with the person you are trying to influence:

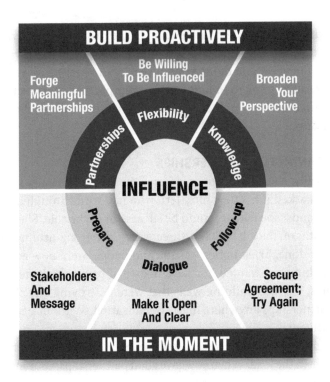

We will look at each of these ingredients individually, but know that for any given situation, you may not need all six. Accomplish the three proactive ingredients well, and the in-the-moment ingredients don't have to be 100% buttoned-down.

But if you don't have the proactive ingredients in place, you will need to nail things in the moment. When trust is not established, you will have to fill the void with a highly effective dialogue.

One point before you read on. This approach is not magic. The magic in it comes from you pulling back on two things you probably rely on right now for influencing—passion and expertise. Passion and expertise convince us that we don't have to do the hard part of influencing—that our idea is so amazing and our expertise backs it, so all we need to do is inform, and they will be on board. That's not how it works. If all that was needed to influence were passion and subject matter expertise, there wouldn't be over 10,000 books on influence currently on Amazon. Influence in organizations is a strategic skill as well as a conversational one, and the approach takes thoughtful planning.

Three Proactive Ingredients

You reap what you sow when influencing in the matrix. The "sowing" includes forging partnerships in your matrix, building trust by demonstrating willingness to be influenced, and doing your homework to make sure you understand what you are attempting to influence from your partner's perspective. These are things you do every day, proactively, to build your overall level of influence in the organization.

FORGE MEANINGFUL PARTNERSHIPS

"Unequivocally, she cannot succeed here," an executive coach told one of my clients when asked if his new hire, Jeri, who had torn through an R&D group leaving the landscape barren, could be successful in the role. She had spent her first six months on the job bullying, threatening and strong-arming project teams to get things done. Trust in her was nil, and people were now actively rallying against anything she wanted, just as a matter of principle. Instead of building partnerships, Jeri was building walls that were destroying any chance she had to build partnerships anywhere in the organization. Without partnerships, she couldn't influence.

A lot of heavy lifting is necessary to get things done in a matrix role, and partnerships lighten the load. When you have good partnerships, your influence grows, not just with the partners, but through them as well. Partners take you at face value and need far less convincing of your motives and the merit of your idea. Integrated and Collaborative Partners are high-trust partnerships. Where there is trust, there is influence. Where there isn't trust, you will need to make investments as outlined in Essential #1 or leverage other parts of the cross-functional influence module.

FLEXIBILITY: BE WILLING TO BE INFLUENCED

In the course I taught at Northwestern, I opened the influence module with a simple question, "Who influences you at work?" Each time I posed that question, I would get at least one student reply with, "No one." These replies exclusively came from students with a lot of letters after their names—well credentialed and not very open to others' influence. Fast forward to the influence course I now teach at the University of Wisconsin, Madison, I pose a different question: "When are you least flexible?" In these courses, the student base is very diverse, but I still see a trend: they consistently report that they are less flexible when they are the expert in the room. Yikes. In my book *Cross-Functional Influence*, I go into this reality in depth. For now, just know that stubborn experts don't have sustainable influence. In order to be influential, you have to be willing to be influenced. Humans are reciprocal animals, and the give and take in organizations is strong.

BUILD YOUR KNOWLEDGE TO BROADEN YOUR PERSPECTIVE

It's no coincidence that the most influential people in the organization are often the most knowledgeable about the organization. And they use that knowledge to guide what they influence, to whom they direct their influence and how they position their ideas. The least influential are those that influence "from the tip of their nose"—influence from their own perspective only, and position their idea in terms of what they want, need or prefer. When you broaden your perspective to see the realities and needs of the people you are influencing, you get heard. When your idea links to something bigger than you (a goal, a strategy or business need), you are more likely to be influential.

Three Ingredients for Influence in the Moment

Next comes your preparation, when you identify your stakeholders and "frame" the issue or idea.

PREPARE: IDENTIFY YOUR STAKEHOLDERS

Back to my class on influence at the University of Wisconsin. I write two phrases on a flipchart on day one—and I go back to these two phrases time and time again. The first is, "Influence is not a straight line." The second is, "Influence is not a solo endeavor." Both of these phrases have to do with stakeholders.

Both phrases really describe the reality that many of our influence opportunities have multiple stakeholders—we don't just simply cook up an idea and go straight to the decision maker to influence. We vet

> *"The greatest ability in business is to get along with others and to influence their actions."*
>
> JOHN HANCOCK

ideas, maybe establish a coalition when we are influencing something big. So when you are thinking about whom you need to influence—err on the safe side and assume you will be influencing more than just one person. Think about your ultimate stakeholder (the decision maker) but also think about others that will need to buy in to your idea or support it in some way.

PREPARE: THINK THROUGH YOUR MESSAGE

The most important message prep you will do is thinking through how you will "frame" your idea. The frame is a 1-3-sentence statement you have in your mind in terms of what the issue is. There are many possible frames for any given issue. Do you frame it as a problem or an opportunity? As an investment or an expense? Do you frame the issue or the solution? A new product to consider or a chance to step into a new market?

Ana, a former colleague of mine, was once given the dubious task of "facilitating" her division's monthly senior leadership meetings with the General Manager (GM) and his 10 direct and dotted line reports (she reported to one of the team members). Everyone except the GM dreaded these meetings; he loved them. Everyone else described them as "talking heads giving updates on stuff that could have been emailed to me." No strategic talk, no problem solving, actually little interaction whatsoever. The team decided "it would be great" if Ana could "fix" the meetings.

She talked to each team member, summarized the feedback and talked to the GM about it. He nodded politely, said he'd think about it, thanked her for her time and stopped just shy of patting her on the head on the way out the door. So she tried a different tack. A week later, she sent him an email framing the situation in financial terms. She calculated the hourly salaries of each leader and then added in travel and other expenses. She changed her frame from "Your people think the time in these meetings could be better spent" to "Did you know you are spending $50,000 per month on these information sharing meetings? Is this your intended investment?" She heard back from him almost immediately. Reframing the problem got his attention. Once she had his attention, the influence was easy.

Jeffrey Pfeffer, in *Managing with Power,* gives a lot of weight to how we frame an issue: "Establishing the framework within which issues will be viewed and decided is often tantamount to determining the result."

We often tend to frame things in one way—our own. Ana framed the meeting issue as she saw it—a problem with the level of engagement. That got her polite disregard. Framing from the recipient's point of view can get their attention right from the start.

Here are the keys to framing the issue or idea you are trying to influence:

Frame the issue in a way that is meaningful to your target. The first thing to do when you are establishing how you will frame the issue is to take the perspective of your target. Rashad tells a great story of influencing people to make difficult personnel decisions:

> *"When I tried to influence new hiring managers to deal with problem performers, I came up against brick walls because they were afraid to hurt someone's feelings. It wasn't until I reframed it away from 'you need to get rid of this problem performer' to 'you need to do what is fair for the other team members that are picking up the slack' that they usually agreed to take action."*

Frame it in a larger context. You have to understand the bigger organizational context before you frame it. Business acumen is a key influence ingredient. Articulate how a change impacts the big picture outside your piece of the matrix. In the leadership-meeting example, Ana initially framed the leadership meetings in terms of what they meant to the participants, which was too narrow for the leader. When she positioned the meetings in the context of his division's investment decisions, she got his attention.

Frame it objectively. One of the leaders involved in this book told a wonderful story of a country manager from Italy. Each time he started down a path he wanted others to follow, he started with, "In my country…" He was given feedback letting him know that this influence tactic wasn't working. Framing it this narrowly, from only his perspective, immediately put others on the defensive and undermined the credibility of his view. Although he changed his wording, he still missed the point. He switched to, "In a country like mine…" To influence in a matrix, when possible, take it out of your personal context. This shows that you are influencing in the right direction and for the right reasons, and it makes your attempt more credible.

THE DIALOGUE: MAKE IT OPEN AND CLEAR

We have talked about the power of inclusion on adopting and implementing decisions—simply put, people adopt decisions quicker and integrate them more fully when they have been involved in them. The same is true of influence. People are

Going in softer, with less defined needs, can work to your advantage in influencing (as well as likely improve your solution).

JUJITSU

more open to influence when you don't come to them with a *fait accompli*. That is not always possible; there are times when you need someone to do something very specific that has no gray around it. But when possible, walk in with some wiggle room and opportunity for them to put their fingerprints on it. Going in softer, with less defined needs, can work to your advantage in influencing (as well as likely improve your solution).

Attempts to influence often create conflict, and people don't have the courage or the appetite for conflict to stay in a conversation. They quit too soon. Keeping yourself and the other person in the dialogue is critical. One matrix leader I talked to called this the organizational equivalent of "never go to bed angry." Keep the conversation going until you both decide to shelve it. Pauses and walk-aways are good, but come back to the issue and make sure you both decide when the exchange is complete.

Let's go back to Ana's conversation with the General Manager about his atrocious meetings. Here are a few things Ana could do to help both of them stay in the conversation:

Keep the relationship front and center. Cross-functional influence requires the relationship to be front and center. Reminding yourself of this changes your tone and the words you choose. Reminding them elevates your dialogue to common ground.

> *"I am committed to being a valuable partner with you on this and the other initiatives we have ahead of us."*

Listen to and acknowledge what they are saying. People who don't feel heard and understood are not open to influence. They shut down or they become defensive of their idea, determined to be heard instead of determined to work with you on the issue. People who are heard open themselves up to influence. Their questions are also valuable, in-the-moment data for you. What are they unclear about? What is holding them back from being influenced? What do they care about? This is exactly the type of information that you need to be influential, and you can't get it if you're talking all the time.

> *"I've heard you mention a couple of times the need you have to connect with people on a monthly basis; I think we can do that and meet some of the other needs they have."*

Restate the big picture and your common ground. When people start to sound defensive or agitated, take a step back and restate what the bigger objective is and what you have in common.

> *"There's no doubt we both want to make sure that the meetings are a strong investment in time and that they help you and the team drive the business."*

State what you are *not* saying. When people feel threatened they may take your comments to the extreme and begin to react to that extreme as opposed to your actual proposition.

> *"I am not suggesting that we scrap everything about the meetings."*

Reinforce your ability to reach agreement. Even when things get contentious, retain your optimism on reaching agreement and communicate that with the person you are talking to.

> *"I think between the two of us we can land on an approach to the meetings that meets your needs and the needs of your team."*

Be clear, succinct, summarize and synthesize. Cross-functional roles and the organizations they reside in are complex, and those who simplify, succeed. I have witnessed, time and again, bright, passionate people with a great idea who drown people in data and fail to influence. Simplicity drives agreement. Reaching an agreement is dependent on your ability to simply and clearly state what is needed and why. If there are options to consider, they must be laid out clearly. Overwhelming already overwhelmed people with a complex description of a problem and its solution undercuts your efforts. If they are going to disagree, you want them to disagree on the merit of your proposal, not because they don't have the energy to figure out what you are requesting.

Simplifying might mean boiling things down into 3 key rationales or a handful of simple options. Visual support helps. Not 10 slides, but 1 table that outlines your cause and effect or options with their pros and cons.

FOLLOW UP: SECURE AGREEMENT OR TRY AGAIN

Not every idea gets traction and sometimes, even when you think you have agreement, no real action takes place. Whether you get nodding heads or shaking heads, your work isn't done.

Scenario 1: No agreement. Rule #1 is don't give up! Two of the most influential clients I have are not the least bit charismatic, but they are respectfully persistent—and that persistence is their super power. If you don't get buy-in, you have three options:

1. Take it to a different stakeholder to gain momentum;

2. Elevate it or delegate to someone else to influence it;

3. Make it more palatable—in other words, make it smaller or less risky, shorten your timeframe or propose a pilot.

Scenario #2: Agreement on your idea. Great news! You've gotten agreement. But your job is not done. Have you ever had a successful influence conversation, walked out of a meeting feeling great, only to see your idea and their commitment evaporate down the line, never to be heard of again? In fast-moving organizations, this happens all the time. Why? Because people have a lot of balls in the air, and they forget. Because they nodded their head but didn't really think you were serious. They got caught up in the moment. Or they agreed, but later changed their mind. Agreements aren't solid; they need follow-up and reinforcement.

You need to make sure that what you just gained agreement on actually sticks:

1. Remind them. Busy people forget. Don't let them. Immediately following the conversation, follow up in person or email, reiterating what you agreed to. Even better if that reminder is a fairly public one—so you have witnesses, so to speak.

2. Reinforce the agreement, make it easy for them. Sometimes the idea is great, but the people get distracted or overwhelmed by what is needed to get it done. Make it easy for them. If you are asking for an additional resource, complete all data entry so all they have to do is hit "approve." If you are asking them to present information on your behalf, put all the slides together. Don't leave the conversation without dates established for a check-in. Ask them what they need from you. Make the process as streamlined and simple as possible for them. Don't let them reject an idea just because it seems like a lot of work.

3. Reward and recognize. This seems basic, but make sure you thank them, even reward them with something or publicly recognize them for what they did. It's a great partnership builder and sets you up for the next time you need to influence. Let's go back to the example of a request for resources. Say you asked for an additional resource and got it. Thank the person in the short term, but also consider six months down the line telling them the impact that this resource had on the project. This reinforces that the two of you made a great decision together and paves the way for the next time you need to tap into that person for a resource, budget or support.

The Power of Patience and Perseverance

Patience may be a virtue, but in a matrix role it is a necessity. In the first edition of *Master the Matrix*, this section on patience and perseverance was just under a page long. I'm about to double that. The pandemic put a whole new spin on many parts of our model, especially the impact of remote work on partnerships, but I also saw it in what and how we influenced and specifically the patience and perseverance that was necessary.

When I sat down with a small team responsible for the return-to-work initiative for a large insurance company, I spent four hours with them diving into their decision-making and their approach to influencing each other and the CEO. I was struck by the patience and finesse they applied in their influence. This working team and the executive-level team had very strong (and well-researched) opinions on the return-to-work approach they favored. It moved slightly as information came out, but their overall opinion stayed pretty darn steady. The CEO held a completely opposing view. I didn't know this going in—I knew about their culture (pretty traditional and hierarchial, title-based, despite in essence being structured as a matrix) and learned all about their impressive efforts. It wasn't until the final hour of my work with them that this reality came out.

I was shocked. Ultimately, they had implemented the approach they were in favor of and the CEO was against. "How on earth did you get him there?" I asked. One team member replied:

"We bought time. We knew we weren't going to win by actively changing his mind: we needed to let things play out. He needed to see what other companies were considering and doing, needed to see numbers in the press and other leaders' responses to them. We knew the trends were in our favor. We just patiently waited for it all to unfold, and he got there."

That's a great example of patience and perseverance at a micro level—specific to an idea. But there's a big picture need for this as well.

You will go home most days feeling like you didn't accomplish anything in all of your attempts to mold and shape those in your matrix. But you did, and if you persist you will see progress. In the opening story for this chapter, Simone said, "It's frustrating to go to work, engage in something I have a lot of passion and pride in and yet have so few victories." I knew from talking to her that she had mastered the matrix more than she realized. But without patience and perseverance, she won't be able to see the progress that she is making.

I was pretty oblivious to the need for these traits well into my career in matrix roles. Then I had a boss, Mary, who changed everything. Mary was a bit of a Zen master. Often I would find myself in influence mode and try to force things— convince the senior leadership team to invest in a project or induce my dotted line corporate boss to change a priority. I

Patience and perseverance are required to see the incremental progress you are making.

MINDSET

would run up against walls over and over again and land in Mary's office frustrated and bruised. "Susan, you are planting seeds," Mary would say. "If you measure your success in days and not months or even years, you are going to go crazy in this role."

One of my upper management interviewees put patience into a great perspective:

> "You have just got to do what is within your control to find the issue, shine a spotlight on it, frame it, present it. What someone else chooses to do with this information is truly above your pay grade—you can't control the big picture, only your role in it. Propose what needs to change, then pin it to somebody's chest, work through it with your boss, whoever. But just keep shining a spotlight on it."

Get good at influencing in a matrix, and you can influence anywhere—it's like New York, if you can make it here, you'll make it anywhere. You are going to see so many things that need to change, improve or go away when you sit at an organizational intersection. Don't let the purview frustrate you—appreciate it and learn to pick and choose where you will make an impact. Your influence abilities, mixed with strong partnerships, underlie every skill, every success you will have in your role. When joined with our next essential, Communicate Without Assumptions, you pack a powerful punch.

IN SUMMARY

EMBRACE

→ The long-term investment that is typical of influence in a matrix—history with people follows you into influence situations. The more positive the history, the higher the likelihood of success.

→ Being influenced, don't just focus on influencing. Your ability to do this increases your influence muscle.

→ The patience and perseverance that is required. Plant seeds and watch for incremental wins, not just the big wins.

WHERE TO START

→ When you are triaging, question your existing boundaries. Try to influence those things that you have previously let go because you didn't think you could impact it. If you have tackled an issue before with mixed results, let it go and see how the situation plays out without your influence.

→ Always think of at least one other frame for something you are influencing. Don't get anchored to the frame that comes to you first—chances are that it is your preferred frame, not your target's.

→ Learn from those who have been influential in your organization (not those with titles, but those who got things done without a big title). Also enlist the help of people who have been able to influence the person you are trying to influence—leverage their knowledge and successes.

IN PRACTICE

FOR LEADERS

Never stop influencing. Even with a big title, it is the best way to build owner-ship and engagement. Be transparent with your influence approach and ob-servations—use them to coach your team. Your insight into how you influence stakeholders across the organization is invaluable to them. Also think of influence in the collective. Yes, individuals on your team have specific skill levels, but in each interaction they are bringing the collective influence of your team/function/loca-tion with them. And their influence can benefit from the position of the team at your level in the organization. Do your peers know what they do and what value they bring? That collective understanding will make people in your organization more influential.

FOR CROSS-FUNCTIONAL/MATRIX TEAMS

Your influence will likely be around accountability in this type of matrix role. Es-sential #7 will cover meetings—these will be your prime influence vehicles. You will likely be influencing a team of people, and meetings can provide motivation and a forum for accountability. Also, when your team needs to influence some-one outside the team, leverage team members. Not all influence needs must be met by you.

WORKING VIRTUALLY

Again, doing anything virtually is bound to take longer, and that includes influ-encing. Doing work individually with stakeholders before you bring them together to influence and decide is helpful. As mentioned earlier, all virtual conversations benefit from visuals, so don't be afraid to use a slide or two even if you are just working with one stakeholder—you aren't being formal, you are being structured and helping to aid focus and clarity. Finally, virtual work can give you tunnel vi-sion and tunnel knowledge. Be disciplined in continuing to build your knowledge outside your immediate area.

> *"Assumptions are the*
> *termites of relationships."*
>
> HENRY WINKLER

ESSENTIAL #6

COMMUNICATE WITHOUT ASSUMPTIONS

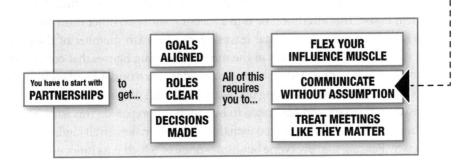

WHAT IT IS

Cross-functional communication is challenging—a constant stream of information needs to be absorbed, analyzed and shared with others in your matrix. To pick up speed we make assumptions on who needs to know what, how they prefer to hear it and even what we ourselves need to know. These assumptions can lead to communication misfires that impact not only your work product but also your trust and credibility.

WHAT THE RESEARCH SAYS

What's most important:
- » Providing information in a way that is easy to understand

What's most likely to trip you up:
- » Knowing what information people need and proactively sharing it
- » Assumption-free listening

PADRAIG is a product owner for an agile development team.

He is in a meeting with his boss and several others from across the matrix, including Aditi, one of his team member's bosses. In the meeting it is announced that they will be adding one more requirement for his project, which will push the deadline back eight weeks—at least one more sprint. Coming out of the meeting, he passes by two project team members and lets them know. That afternoon he is in a meeting with two other team members and lets both of them know. That leaves Mark, the sixth member of the team. Mark reports to Aditi, who was in the meeting. Padraig figures that connection will ensure Mark is informed, so he doesn't need to reach out. A few days later, the team convenes and starts working out a new plan, with the new deadline. Mark is confused, in the dark and frustrated to be caught unprepared. This isn't the first time he has been caught flat-footed with this team. He makes up all kinds of stories about why Padraig told everyone but him—none of which is as innocuous as the simple assumption Padraig made. Eventually all Mark's assumptions start to show up in how he communicates with the team—how much he shares, how engaged he is. The team reacts by retracting as well.

Padraig fell into a trap that is common to matrix roles. To streamline a messy matrix he made all kinds of assumptions and got himself in all kinds of trouble. Drawn out, this assumption cycle looks something like this:

Caught in this vortex, our communication becomes based more on assumption than fact, and things can go downhill fast. This cycle can happen in any context, but even more so in matrix roles because of the sheer number of people we interact with and messages we are bombarded with. Mixed, incomplete and garbled messages are inevitable. Several leaders I talked to compared communication in a matrix to the game "Telephone," where the message starts out crystal clear to the initiator, is passed along from person to person and ends in a jumbled mess.

Consider this visual comparison of communication in traditional roles versus in a matrix role:

TRADITIONAL ROLE   MATRIX ROLE

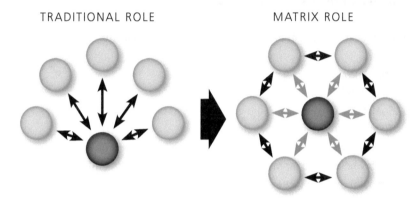

In a matrix not only do you have more people to communicate with (more circles, as shown above), you also have some interest in and even responsibility for the communication that takes place *between* the people in your matrix (just like Padraig in the opening story). This multidirectional, once-removed communication makes things especially challenging.

All these extra circles and arrows lead us to look for shortcuts, and that's where assumptions come in. Assumptions are everywhere. If we acted without them, we would never get anything done—we would always be waiting for the full picture to appear before taking a step. But often, the time these assumptions save up front is negated by time spent later making amends and resolving miscommunications. These shortcuts catch up with you.

Often you won't even realize that you are operating on an assumption until someone does or says something in direct conflict with that assumption. About three conversations into my relationship with my book designer, he provided printing price quotes and gave me examples of a lot of terrific booklets under 100 pages. In the tote sitting next to me, I had brought examples of 200-page hardcover business books I admired. How did we get that far into a project with such divergent assumptions? My assumption was so ingrained that I didn't even know I had it—I didn't even think of telling him!

I am going to make a big, sweeping counterintuitive statement about cross-functional communication: *assumptions, not skills, are the biggest barriers to effective communication.* As a more intuitive follow-up declaration: *trust is predicated on communication.* Challenge your assumptions, improve your communication and grow your trust. If you don't cultivate trust, cross-functional roles simply do not work, or they collapse under the weight of all the processes and policies needed to make them work, as we learned in Essential #1.

Assumptions and What They Lead To

So, here's how it goes. You are moving fast and you assume:

- » They know.
- » They don't know.
- » Somebody else already told them.
- » They don't need to know.
- » I'm the one to tell them.
- » I know how to tell them (or it doesn't matter how I tell them).
- » I know the whole picture.

These assumptions—and all their variations—cause us to make a number of blunders in matrix roles. We often find ourselves:

- » Undercommunicating
- » Overcommunicating
- » Communicating to the wrong people
- » Communicating in the wrong way
- » Not listening

And the result is:

- » Perceptions of information hoarding, politicking and other suspicions
- » Confusion
- » Lack of information or misinformation

These outcomes all lead to lack of trust, which means slower decision-making, decreased decision quality and less influence for you.

Let's take a look at the risks and remedies for each of these missteps.

Undercommunicating

Rebecca was an academic researcher who transferred to a corporate role advising pharmaceutical research. She went from one of the most independent roles out there to a matrix, dependent on and connected to many, many others. Communication was her nemesis. She continually undercommunicated because she thought people knew, didn't need to know or that the reasons behind her actions and decisions were inherently obvious. The researchers and academics she was surrounded by in her previous life had low information needs beyond what was in front of them—she was the expert and they followed her lead. Now she was surrounded by people who needed to know what was going on inside her head, and she wasn't sharing it readily, if at all.

Rebecca quickly found out that in matrix roles, people have higher information needs—period. Overlapping roles and goals, ambiguity and close collaboration all increase the appetite for information. Those in your matrix will need to know more than your peers in a traditional organization might.

Rebecca's failure to broadcast brought on many unintended consequences that are prevalent among undercommunicators:

» People around her filling in the blanks themselves (and acting upon them)
» Rebecca or others making decisions downstream without all the information
» People finding out information from others and feeling duped
» Others caught flat-footed when they are approached with the information

There are four things to keep in mind in terms of the communication needs of others: (1) they don't know what you know; (2) you don't necessarily know what they need to know; (3) the reason behind your actions is important to people and not inherently obvious and (4) when asked for information, your response matters.

THEY DON'T KNOW WHAT YOU KNOW

Whether it is expertise acquired over time or information acquired day to day, it's tough to appreciate what you know that others don't. Brian, a consultant to matrix organizations, put it best:

> "There are few things harder than knowing what it's like to _not_ know what you know. And therefore, you assume that other people must know it."

This is made tougher by the fact that we often assume someone else is communicating to the people in our matrix—just like the story of Padraig and Mark. Remember the extra arrows that represented communication between the people in your matrix? They often fall apart. Both your solid line boss and your dotted line boss attend the same weekly leadership team meeting. That means they talk, right? So if you tell one, that message gets through to the other, right? Wrong. You are in a meeting with the manager of one of the people in your "hub." Important information on an upcoming customer visit is shared. Your hub member's boss will tell her, right? Probably not—that boss is probably making the same assumption about you!

Regardless of what drives your assumption of someone else's knowledge, you have to flip the switch and go from assuming they know to assuming they don't. Here's a great analogy. My oldest daughter played fast-pitch softball. During her first year of true competitive play, the pitchers were

You have to shift from assuming they know to assuming they *don't*, and communicate accordingly.

MINDSET

much better and much faster than she was accustomed to. She was in a serious batting slump, and assumptions were partially to blame. She was used to pitchers who rarely threw strikes—so at the plate she assumed that the pitch coming at her was a ball and would only talk herself into swinging if it happened to be a strike. But these girls threw more accurately and faster, which meant that her assumption didn't work—pitches were flying right past her and into the catcher's glove before she could decide to swing. She had to switch her assumption from "it will be a ball" to "it will be a strike" in

As information comes in, always ask yourself "Who needs to know?"

TRIAGE

order to make contact with the ball. In other words, changing her assumption made her much more successful.

This mental shift is the same one we have to make in our cross-functional work—from assuming they know to assuming they don't, and that *not* communicating (like watching a pitch go by) is the exception rather than the rule. This means that with every bit of information coming toward you, your first question should always be, "Who needs to know?"

YOU DON'T NECESSARILY KNOW WHAT THEY NEED TO KNOW

Sometimes we undercommunicate because we don't think another person needs to know. Rebecca truly couldn't understand why in the world anyone would care about her work. After all—it was *her* work.

What makes us think that we are experts in the information needs of others?

Remember the last time you walked out of your boss's office with marching orders, only to find out that what you just committed to doing by the end of the day required more information than you had at your fingertips? If you don't always have a firm grasp on your *own* information needs, why would you assume you have it for someone else's?

If...	Then...
You are in a meeting	In the margins note what you will need to communicate, to whom and how after the meeting
You get an email with information	Think "forward" not just "reply"
You have multiple stakeholders that connect	Don't assume they talk; leave nothing to chance (better they hear it twice than not at all)
You are in doubt as to their need to know	When in doubt, shout it out

Don't guess at another person's information needs—ask them. Information needs are not immediately obvious in a matrix. When you can, plan. Set up a process with your partner that ensures you are sharing pertinent information in the most effective and efficient way. There are going to be far more people to get messages out to, so you have got to become efficient at this. Establish a quick way to identify who needs to know and get out the information. Making this practice part of your continual, in-the-moment thought process and executing it with discipline will make you more effective and efficient. An engineer on six different projects had a cheat sheet and corresponding email distribution list for each of the projects he was on: "I just made it automatic, so it was easy to get out and just part of my process."

YOUR "WHY" IS NOT OBVIOUS

We assume that people inherently know and appreciate the reason behind our actions and decisions. Why is he here for a visit? Why is she asking these questions about the project plan? Why did he decide to bring in a consultant? Why did she push back the deadline?

Why, indeed. Our actions make perfect sense to us (or at least they should!). Inside our heads, the steps we took and our full rationale is laid out. The problem is that no one else can see inside our heads. In a cross-functional role this becomes increasingly dangerous because of the number of people who are involved and the corresponding stories they can make up and propagate about the rationale behind your actions.

If remembering to communicate the "what" of your knowledge is challenging (as per the previous section), then the "why" doubles down on that challenge. We assume the "why" is inherently obvious, but it rarely is. People are smart, and the "what" alone isn't enough for them. They need to know the "why." If they don't, they will fill in the blanks.

We tend to attribute our decisions and actions to positive intent. But as for the decisions and actions of others, we lean more toward assuming the worst. David Grossman, Founder and CEO of the communication consultancy The Grossman Group, says it best:

> *"Given two ways to interpret what's behind an action or decision, people inevitably choose the most harmful of the choices."*

So be as readily transparent and forthright with the "why" behind your actions as you are with the "what." Don't make them guess—believe me, you won't like their guess!

How can we stop ourselves from making the assumption that they know our intentions? Here are a few options:

- Provide the complete picture and context. Use the journalist's rule of covering the who, what, why and when.

- Don't wait for them to ask why—give the information up front.

- When asked "why," assume they are curious, not questioning, and answer in a way that encourages future "why" questions and discourages filling in the blanks.

WHEN PEOPLE ASK, YOUR RESPONSE MATTERS

A supply chain manager told me about a person who worked for her. His biggest failing in his matrix role? Taking questions too personally. He took every question as a personal affront to his skills, experience and effectiveness. Ultimately, it cost him his job.

The increased information appetite when working cross-functionally means more questions. Take them for what they are—don't personalize, don't take offense, don't assume they are trying to disprove your expertise. Answer questions with patience and sincerity—regardless of how others respond in return. In a matrix, you

Answer questions with patience and sincerity— regardless of how others respond in return.

JUJITSU

accomplish things with and through other people and that requires dialogue. And that dialogue includes questions. If you take questions personally, you won't get very far, because your defensiveness will show and affect the level of trust that people have in you.

A government affairs manager I worked with thought of questions as a positive challenge. She put it this way:

> *"I see it as my personal challenge to make sure they are in the know. Whenever they have to ask for an update, I ask myself, 'OK, where did I blow it? What was I assuming?' My goal is to never have them ask for something I should have given them automatically."*

Overcommunicating

Kristoph was a new director of facilities who moved from a small, privately held company to a large corporation. I was brought in to coach him on his transition—which was not going well at all. I spoke to about 10 people he worked with—employees, partners, bosses. One theme came out loud and clear. He wasn't communicating enough—everyone felt in the dark. I gave him the feedback, and we discussed ideas on how to improve. Six weeks later, I circled back to the people I talked to. Their new complaint? He was flooding them with emails and updates, and they were drowning in information.

Kristoph's lesson was that simply swinging the pendulum from undercommunicating to sharing every tidbit of information you get with your entire email distribution list is not really the answer. In today's world of information overload, you can't just add to the avalanche of information. People feel overcommunicated with when you provide a lot of information that:

» Is perceived as irrelevant to their needs
» Isn't user friendly to get through
» Appears self-serving in nature

Some people think the key to successful cross-functional communication is the "Cc" field and the "Forward" button on their computer. But simply forwarding information on is often not enough. Here are a few steps you should take to ensure that you are hitting the right balance in your communication:

From the get-go	Ask: What information can I share on an ongoing basis that would be helpful?
	Ask: What is the best way to provide it?
In the message	Tell: Here's why I am sharing this with you.
	Tell: Here's the information that is most important.
	Ask: Was this information helpful? Is this the kind of information I should continue to send your way?
	Cc: Only those who really need to know, and let people know why they are Cc'd.
Ongoing	Ask: Are you getting what you need from me? What information is most helpful? Least?

I was reviewing this chart with a group when a woman raised her hand: "Susan, great chart, but I don't possibly have the time to tell my email recipients why I am sharing and what's most important." I politely asked her if she assumed that her recipients had the time to figure it out for themselves. Stopping the avalanche of email is a team effort.

Overcommunication happens in live form as well—but often less so, because we can self-correct in real time. Watch for cues such as eye contact, nodding and questions or statements that directly relate to what you are saying. Over the phone, focus on the verbal cues such as relevant questions and statements. An absence of these cues might mean that you have communicated completely but excessively or that they don't perceive the information as important enough to listen to and form questions or comments around.

In person, on video or over the phone, be very, very conscious of the balance of dialogue. If it's not 50/50, pull back. Let them ask questions to guide the discussion—don't think you have to answer everything before they have a chance to ask a question. Monologues (another form of overcommunicating) don't come close to the productivity of dialogues.

Overcommunicating is still less risky for trust building than information hoarding in a matrix role. Kristoph's incessant forwarding and updating annoyed people, but they didn't doubt his motives. On the other hand, in Rebecca's case, her undercommunication led to speculation and stories, creating a dynamic that took months to mend. Let them tell you (or even better, outright ask them) if the information is unnecessary. But don't assume.

Let them ask questions to guide the discussion—don't think you have to answer everything before they have a chance to ask a question.

JUJITSU

Cast a Wide Net: Communicating with the Right People

Two realities of cross-functional work should challenge your assumptions about "who needs to know." The first we have already talked about—information appetites are higher. Not only do people need to know more, but more people need to know. The second is that to some extent the matrix neutralizes titles and levels. Who you interact with doesn't always line up with your title. I talked to people who led projects with team members one or two titles up, even a few who led teams on which their own boss was a team member. You may partner on equal ground with someone two steps below and in another function.

You will also find yourself a target of communication from many different directions. All bets are off in matrix organizations regarding the hierarchy of who talks to whom. Get used to it, and don't let the organizational chart be your guide to whom to communicate to and whom to receive communication from.

These realities mean you will have to cast a wider net in your communication. More people will need to know and you will be the one expected to tell them—regardless of your level or theirs. One engineer and project manager put it this way, "I just figure out how many people I think need to know and then double that—it gets me in the ballpark." He was being facetious, but you do need to push yourself on who needs to know and realize that there are probably more than you think.

You will always have to cast a wider net in your communication than you initially assume. **ZOOM OUT**

Not only do cross-functional roles require a wider net of communication, they also challenge the traditional assumption that your boss is your most important audience. He or she is not. As a matter of fact, your boss may need to know significantly less and at a significantly lower level of detail than others in your matrix. More than likely, the real work gets done through communicating everywhere but up. Of course your boss shouldn't be in the dark, but he/she is not your only audience or at times your most important audience. When I review multisource (360) feedback with matrix leaders, it is almost always the peers and subordinates who feel the most in the dark. The motivation to communicate with your boss may be clear, while the motivation to communicate with those around you may be less so. But placing too great an emphasis on communicating up is a mistake—not only will others in your matrix be less informed than they need to be, but they will also make assumptions about the reasons behind your focus on upward communication.

To ensure that you are both balanced and complete in your communication to your matrix, make sure you think about the following:

- Know who does what so you know where to direct communication.

- Use visual cues to help you remember whom you need to get certain messages to (project team lists, email lists, etc.).

- Push yourself to think of one more person when you think your list is complete.

- When in doubt, shout it out.

- Beware of the "out of sight/out of mind" communication trap—take extra steps to communicate to those who are not colocated with you. Especially true in our more virtual work world.

Yours Is Not Theirs: Communicating in the Right Way

Figuring out how to communicate is where the diversity of the people in the matrix really becomes obvious. The more you interact outside of your immediate functional area, the fewer assumptions you can make about a person's communication preferences and level of understanding. In your corner of the world, people may share preferences and levels of expertise—to the point that you may appear to be "talking in code" to others. When venturing outside your corner, those assumptions can get you in trouble.

UNDERSTAND THEIR PREFERENCES
We tend to give what we want to get in communication. If we prefer email, we email everyone; if we like face to face, we assume everyone does; if we like to jump right into details, then that's how we deliver information to others.

Here's a great example of assuming your communication preference is theirs:

Maria to Susan:
Those long text summaries you leave me at the end of the day drive me absolutely crazy—can you just drop me texts on single issues?

Susan to Eduardo:
Those top-of-mind emails you leave me throughout the day drive me nuts—can you just leave me a summary at the end of the day?

Yes, those were actual conversations from my boss to me and then from me to one of my employees. In both cases, Eduardo and I were assuming that our individual communication preferences (for me, it was a "daily digest" and for him it was single-topic messages) were also the preferences of our bosses.

There are as many communication preferences as there are people to have them. The point is not to create custom messages around every person in your matrix. But when the stakes are high or when you are working with someone on an ongoing basis, preferences matter. Get to know the preferences of the key people in your matrix—what do they need to know and how do they want to receive it? Don't assume they like to hear it the same way you do. This helps ensure your message doesn't misfire because of the way it was delivered.

With partners you will work with on an ongoing basis, get some of these preferences out on the table. A few questions to ask:

- What kinds of information do you prefer via email, text or in person?

- Where's the best starting point for a discussion? Are you a "Give me the bottom line, and I will ask questions" type, or do you prefer I start at the beginning with all the details?

- When's the best time to catch you live? Do you mind drop-bys, or would you rather I set up time formally?

UNDERSTAND WHAT THEY UNDERSTAND

Another trap we fall into is having our expertise cloud how we deliver a message. In sharing that expertise we can sometimes assume they know—and talk way over their heads—or assume they don't know and condescend to the point of distraction.

The matrix brings a variety of expertise together to reach a common goal. But all that expertise can be underutilized if everyone talks like they would back in their home base. Being able to translate technical expertise—be it financial, scientific, operational, etc.—is becoming as important as having the expertise in the first place. Not only using language that is jargon-free but stopping to define jargon that is especially critical to understanding

"If you talk to a man in a language he understands, that goes to his head. If you talk to him in his language, that goes to his heart."

NELSON MANDELA

is a daily requirement in a matrix role. Contextualizing technical information through examples and stories is also important. To communicate technical information effectively in your matrix you must not only be clear but connect the information to your audience.

What you don't need to do is preface all your technical explanations. Helen, an engineer, was partnering with Tomas, an IT leader, on the implementation of a new electronic process for project tracking. Tomas had a habit of starting conversations off with "You probably don't realize it, but…" As a well-educated, highly successful engineer, Helen didn't take too kindly to this—especially after she began a master's degree in an IT-related field. As she tells the story, "I couldn't wait for an opportunity to pounce on his comment and tell him how much I really did understand and realize all that he was talking about." Tom's assumptions got in the way of Helen trusting him and working with him—she started to shut him out.

It's hard to strike a balance between sharing in layman's terms and not coming off as condescending. It's also hard to appreciate and translate your expertise or to stop yourself from jumping in when you know you have the technical expertise and they don't. You are going to be faced with this a lot when working cross-functionally—again, that is the point of a matrix, bringing together a diversity of expertise.

In either case—assuming they know or don't know, here are a few ways to keep your expertise in check:

Rule of thumb	What it sounds like
Provide expertise without arrogance or impatience.	"Stop me if this is redundant or if I am telling you something you already know," "What else can I answer?"
Ask if they are interested in learning more.	"Is this helpful? Should I keep going?"
Find out what they know by asking questions (in a nonthreatening way).	"What would be most helpful for you to know? I don't want to bore you with details that aren't important."
Provide information in layman's terms and check to see if you slipped in any jargon.	"I'm close to this, so it is second nature to me—Did I explain that clearly? Any technical terms that I breezed by?"

Assumption-Free Listening

Our focus so far has been on how we communicate out. But assumptions can also affect the way we take in information. Think about how you listen when the topic is one you know well versus one that is new. Right now you may be skimming this chapter because you feel saturated with "how-tos" on communication—what could this chapter offer that is new and different? When we assume we have the full picture, we stop really listening (or in this case reading)—when we aren't curious, our brains move on to other topics.

When working cross-functionally, listening is the bridge between your expertise and those of the people in your matrix. Without listening to each other, you are just two experts on parallel paths who may never meet to create what is intended.

However, this doesn't mean you have to listen with the intent of understanding everything around you. I distinctly remember the meetings I sat through in my first foray into a matrix role. I was very used to projects and corresponding meetings that fell directly into my area of expertise. All of the sudden I was in meetings where I didn't understand 95% of what they were talking about. I would take copious notes on all the terms, acronyms and concepts that I didn't know and bring them back to my boss for answers. She would patiently answer what she could. After several of these Q&A sessions, she said to me, "Susan, you aren't expected to know all of this—that's not your role. The point is not for you to be as expert as them, it is to pull out what you need to do your job." To her credit, telling me that (as well as being unafraid to demonstrate that she didn't know all of it either) helped me put what I needed to understand in perspective.

Assumption-free listening is about realizing you don't have the full picture, asking genuine questions when you need to and actually absorbing the answers you receive. Jada, a customer service leader, learned this lesson the hard way after coming into a new matrix and "assuming that they hadn't thought of any of this and that's why they brought me in." After more than a few missteps and a few months of repair work, her mantra became, "Appreciate what happened before you got here."

I would add that it is not only "what happened before you got here" but also "what happens when you're not here." Whether it is a new project or a new person or team you are working with, you only have a small slice of the information on their history, role and responsibilities. Don't assume it is anything more than a small slice. A little listening with curiosity and humility goes a long way toward not only gathering useful information for your problem solving and decision-making, but also in building the partnership.

Assumptions stop us from hearing anything that doesn't match up with what

> You don't have to listen with the intent of understanding everything around you; learn to let some information go.
>
> **TRIAGE**

we hold in our heads, and they stop us from being curious and asking questions. When you walk in without assumptions, you're automatically going to be a better questioner and listener. For assumption-free listening, keep these things in mind:

Ask two more questions. Even when you think you know the person, find two questions to ask them about themselves. When you think you know all the nuances of the problem, ask two more questions. Think you get all the ramifications of the solution? Ask two more questions.

Ask questions like a three-year old. Why, Why, Why. Any parent of a young child will tell you that the "Why" stage is both exciting (because it shows their intellectual growth) and frustrating (because it can be all-consuming, and you don't have the all the answers). Asked with genuine curiosity, the question of "Why" is a great assumption breaker, especially when you think you already know the answer. Just make sure you ask the "why" without the "whine."

Don't match their defense with more defense. People are not used to being asked questions—they are used to people assuming and doing. So when you start asking questions, you may get a little defense from them in return. That's ok; the only thing you can do is to keep your tone non-defensive and express your (genuine) appreciation for taking time to answer your questions.

Keep your tone non-defensive and express your (genuine) appreciation for taking time to answer your questions.

JUJITSU

Absorb it. All of this inquisitiveness doesn't do much good if you don't absorb and apply the information you acquire. The first step to absorbing it is simply restating it. Restating helps you mentally register the information (far more than just hearing it) and tells the other person that you heard them. As a further step, add a "so that's why" at the end to connect the dots between their answer and your experience. For example, if you ask a person in your hub how requests are prioritized, respond to their answer by adding: "OK, so that's why when I ask for customer return data I hear back pretty quickly, but the lead time on contract changes is longer."

Cross-functional work is built around complex projects with lots of history and complex problems with many tentacles. You partner with people who have different experiences and styles. Nothing is straightforward, including your communication. Be prepared for this—realizing the challenges can help you turn off your assumptions. Once your assumptions are disabled, your communication and listening skills can fully develop and ultimately drive your results. And you will need all of those communication and listening faculties as you enter the realm of matrix meetings, which is the focus of Essential #7.

IN SUMMARY

EMBRACE

→ The higher-than-usual information needs of people in the matrix

→ People asking you a lot of questions about your work

→ The risk of overcommunicating

→ The communication styles and preferences of your partners

→ What you don't know—be an assumption-free listener

WHERE TO START

→ When you get information, the first thing you should ask is, who needs to know this?

→ When you participate in a meeting, note everything that you will need to share with someone after the meeting in the margins or italics. Then you can easily skim your notes and identify what to communicate and to whom.

→ Challenge yourself to stay one step ahead of people on updates. If your boss beats you to the punch and asks you for an update, figure out why— did you think they knew? Didn't need to know? File that away for next time.

→ Even when you think you know a person, find two questions to ask them about themselves. When you think you know all the nuances of the problem, ask two more questions. Think you get all the ramifications of the solution? Ask two more questions.

→ Set up a rhythm for your communication. People trust communication that comes out consistently in terms of content, timing and format. They trust that they are getting the full story and become really good at grabbing the information they need.

IN PRACTICE

FOR LEADERS

The biggest assumption that trips a leader up is assuming your team heard the first time and understood. As mentioned in the goal alignment chapter, there is power in the repeated, consistent message. Common advice is that when you get really sick of communicating a message, it is just starting to stick in the minds of others. Also, watch your assumptions on how much you need to know. As you grow in an organization, your information needs are not cumulative. Be realistic about what you really need to know and conscious of how your information needs impact behaviors in your team.

FOR CROSS-FUNCTIONAL/MATRIX TEAMS

Your key challenge in this type of role is translation. You will have to make sure that critical technical information is shared and absorbed effectively. If you are leading the team, take frequent pauses to allow questions or even better pose the questions yourself. This shows team members that it is OK not to understand all of the information on the first pass. If you are a team member, don't be afraid to ask the question—don't assume you are the only one with that question, because chances are you are not.

WORKING VIRTUALLY

The danger of assumptions is doubled when working virtually. Listening, under-standing and memory are all impacted when your main mode is virtual. In addition, beware of defaulting to email. Email is a transactional information-sharing tool that creates Transactional Partnerships. As old school as it sounds—pick up the phone once in a while. The illusion of the speed that email provides is just that—an illusion. Face to face, face to screen or voice to voice are where the speed can be found.

ESSENTIAL #7
MAKE MEETINGS MATTER

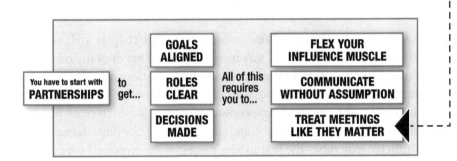

WHAT IT IS

Like relationships, meetings are not separate from results—they are *how* results are achieved in matrix roles. Get really good at meetings, and you will have better partnerships and be more influential. The results will follow.

WHAT THE RESEARCH SAYS

What's most important:
» Only calling meetings when absolutely necessary

What's most likely to trip you up:
» Following up after meetings and holding people accountable

YOU will be tempted to skip this chapter. You have heard it all before—you know what it takes to run a meeting. Or maybe you think you are too junior or too senior to worry about this skill. WAKE UP! In a cross-functional role, regardless of your level, meetings are absolutely, positively critical—this is where the pieces of the matrix actually come together. You have to get them right or your matrix will splinter. Read on…

I am sitting here in Delavan, Wisconsin, writing this chapter and, as usual, I started with the research. And I screamed. Because what does my research say about meetings? As a category and as individual questions, it ranks as the least important aspect of working cross-functionally. How can we simultaneously complain about so many meetings, know that nothing we do in cross-functional organizations is purely independent, and yet STILL not place importance on them?

I distinctly remember the first matrix project team meeting I ever attended. Prior to walking into the meeting my boss told me, "Wait 'til you meet Pete, the project lead, he leads the best meeting I have ever been in."

I brushed the remark off, determined not to be impressed, for I, too, was known to lead a pretty decent meeting.

But what I saw in that conference room that day blew me away. Here was this guy, laid back, unassuming—I didn't even know he was the project lead until he kicked off the meeting—who led a meeting like I had never seen before. He was a master. It was like my career to date had been comprised of black and white, and I was just introduced to HD.

He laid out the plan for the meeting, he called people out, he connected dots, he challenged, he pulled us back from tangents and pulled us out of the forest so that we could see the trees. At the end he was able to present back a neat summary of where we had been, what we decided and who was on the hook for what for the next meeting. He was able to take all this raw material that we brought in and turn it into a real work product.

I walked out of the meeting completely pumped to be part of the project. I felt like we could take on the world. Heck, I felt like I personally could take on the world. He took this behemoth of a project stretching multiple oceans and functional lines and simplified it, made it doable.

Until you have been in a meeting like that, you don't see the potential for power. Motivation and influence are two key requirements in matrix roles, and meetings can be your tool. In a matrix role, meetings are the forum for avoiding and resolving collisions and producing results by bringing together divergent goals, opinions and experiences.

The meetings that are convened in matrix roles are definitely not run-of-the-mill meetings—there is so much at stake. They are the most visible, public display of your abilities to work cross-functionally. They give you the potential to motivate through inclusion and build ownership where you can't motivate through incentives or authority. We spend time and invest dollars trying to reward, recognize and ultimately motivate people. What motivates people? Getting stuff done. Friends, peers and camaraderie also motivate people. Do you know where you get stuff done while simultaneously surrounding yourself with friends, peers and comrades? Meetings! Meetings have great potential. But that potential is seldom realized.

As discussed in Essential #5, your formal power is limited in a matrix role, but the need to influence is seemingly unlimited. Do you know where you can build influence? You guessed it: a meeting. Show people you are disciplined and can drive to a result while respecting their time, and you become an influencer.

It Starts with the Right Mindset

The title of this Essential really says it all concerning the mindset that is absolutely necessary—*meetings matter*. Valuing meetings as the powerful, productive, motivating force that they really can and should be should come before any agenda or meeting management tactic you employ. Placing a value on meetings transforms them from an interruption to a critical function and opportunity. With this assumption in mind, the time you put in up front shifts—you put more in and voila! You get more out.

Meetings matter; give them the treatment they deserve.

MINDSET

MEETINGS ARE NOT A DEPARTURE FROM WORK, THEY ARE YOUR WORK

"I was in meetings all day, I didn't get anything done." How often have you heard or said that? The first thing we need to do is shift that way of thinking. Meetings that are called for the right reason and managed in the right way (both of which we will talk about later) are not an intrusion on your productivity; they are the vehicle for your productivity. This is especially true in a matrix role—meetings are the "cross" in cross-functional; it's where you all come together. Without them the matrix fragments.

Meetings have become a caricature of themselves. It is much more entertaining to complain about a really bad meeting than rave about one that was superproductive. But if we stop thinking about meetings as if they are vast conspiracies to hijack precious work time, the rest of the mindsets and skills will fall into place.

YOU GET OUT OF MEETINGS WHAT YOU PUT INTO THEM

Jeanine is pulling 10 people together to talk about data she collected on a customer visit. She is stretched to the max and doesn't have an hour prior to the meeting to plan it, but she figures everybody has the general gist of what needs to happen. She walks into the meeting and spends the first 20 minutes going over why everyone is here and what they are going to discuss. They get into the conversation and the hour is up. So she schedules another meeting to finish things up. She walks into meeting #2 and starts by refreshing everyone's memory about what they covered last time, why she wanted to talk about it in the first place and where the conversation left off. This catch-up eats up 30 minutes. They get into the meat of the topic and then the meeting is over. So what does she do? Jeanine decides that next time they need to meet for two hours instead of one!

Jeanine is getting out of these meetings exactly what she is putting in: nothing. A one-hour meeting is turning into a four-hour meeting with no end in sight. Too bad she didn't have that one hour up front to think it through.

If meetings really matter, put in the time beforehand to really think them through—desired outcomes and structured agenda are a given. By doing this, we end the meeting death spiral—one bad meeting whose only outcome is to create another bad meeting.

Six Steps to Meetings That People Actually Want to be Part of

Your success or failure at leading a meeting starts well before you have the group in the room. The thought and planning that goes into a meeting can make or break its success. Nothing in the moment—during the meeting—can make up for lack of planning on the front end.

The six steps outlined here are not optional or nice to have. They are required. This is what it looks like to *treat meetings like they matter*. You need to be diligent in these steps, whether you are planning a one-hour meeting or a one-week meeting.

The Six Steps:

1. Attempt to talk yourself out of it
2. Get really clear on your outcomes
3. Craft your agenda
4. Invite and prepare the right people
5. Facilitate the heck out of it
6. Follow up and hold people accountable

Step I. Attempt to Talk Yourself out of It

Let's go back to Jeanine. She had some customer data that she wanted to "tell people about." Before going any further, she needs to try to talk herself out of it. Meetings should be the exception, not the rule. Don't let "call a meeting" be your default, give it some critical thought. Not sure if you should have the meeting? Ask the people you would invite to attend. Do they think a meeting is necessary?

Some good reasons to hold a meeting include: solve a problem, brainstorm ideas, make a decision, plan/create. Some bad reasons include: discuss, explore, share information. So for Jeanine, wanting to "talk about customer data" may not be a good reason to hold a meeting, unless she can answer affirmatively to one of these questions:

- Is the information urgent and they must hear it from you, either because it is sensitive or you are the only messenger who can or should deliver it?

  An example of this would be a major personnel announcement.

- Does the message need to be delivered to a set of people at the same time for consistency of message and to prevent any "leaking" of your message?

  A major announcement like a project cancellation would fall into this category.

- Is the information not self-explanatory, or would making it self-explanatory take more time and effort than is warranted?

  If Jeanine's customer information was so complex that it couldn't stand alone, she would want to hold an information-sharing meeting.

Always consider your options to a meeting—alternative forms of communication, one-to-one conversations, etc. Never assume that a meeting is the answer. People's time is valuable, and meetings are a really expensive way to share information.

> Never assume a meeting is the answer; consider your options.
>
>
>
> **MINDSET**

Step 2. Get Very, Very Specific on Outcomes

I truly don't believe that people wake up one morning and say, "You know what, I am going to call a meeting next week that has absolutely no purpose and is a complete waste of time." I'm sure Jeanine-with-the-customer-data didn't roll out of bed thinking this way. Each meeting holds some nugget of value—an important question that needs to be answered, some problem that needs to be solved. However, many times we do a really good job of hiding it. Maybe this is because we think its value is self-evident, or we sense that there is a purpose but can't put our finger on it?

Remember Ana back in Essential #5 who was trying to influence the horrible senior leadership meetings? The General Manager had a vague sense of what he wanted to get out of the meetings, which is fine if you are having a one-hour business lunch with someone. But when you are pulling multiple people together for a long period of time and, in this case, from around the world, you have to get specific.

Think about why you want to pull the meeting together. Write it down; don't just get a general sense of why you need to have it. Get specific and be prepared to answer the question in a sentence or two (because you will have to answer it in a sentence or two when people question the need for the meeting).

Differentiating between what I call *outcome verbs* and *talk verbs* is really important when you are thinking about a meeting's outcome. Here's the difference:

The purpose of this meeting is to…

Outcome Verbs	*Talk Verbs*
Resolve	Discuss
Decide	Explore
Identify	Share
Create	Confer

The first list lends itself to physical manifestation. This is a good bias. What will be lying on the table at the end of the meeting? An answer to a question? A decision? A plan? A list of prioritized issues? Even if it won't literally be a physical product, if you think of it this way, it is easier to form your agenda and ultimately direct the conversation. Discussion, exploration and sharing may also happen, but they are not your ultimate goal.

If your goal does not fit neatly into this first list, go back to Step 1 and attempt to talk yourself out of it. There are probably other ways to make this happen, or at least ways to begin information sharing so that you can move quickly into the next phase (i.e., resolve, decide, etc.). If there isn't a next phase, you need to question why they need the information at all.

Your outcome is the starting point for your agenda. Let's go back to Jeanine and her meeting on customer data. Notice that she started with the need to "talk about the data." For Jeanine, like everyone else, talk verbs are not great when Nick Naysayer is on the invite list. When Nick calls and asks, "What is this meeting all about? Do we really need it?" and Jeanine replies with "We are going to talk about..." she makes it easy for Nick to discount the meeting (and accidently double-book himself or multitask during the meeting). If Jeanine is able to respond with a solid meeting outcome like, *"The purpose of the meeting is to review customer data and decide what we will act on and when,"* her rationale is much more powerful, and the chance of Nick making the meeting a priority increases.

Step 3. Craft Your Agenda (Hint: It Is Not a List of Topics)

If the #1 no-no is calling a meeting without an agenda, then the follow-up no-no is providing a lame agenda—a list of topics to cover. An agenda is much more than this. If you only have a list of topics to cover, go back to Step 1 and consider alternatives to a meeting.

Your agenda should take your participants from point A to point B to their final destination: the outcome you identified in the previous step. The agenda represents the *thought process* you are going to take them through to reach your end point. It is also a visual aid for your participants. You are most likely competing with others in the matrix for their attention, so your agenda better look like it is setting up for high-impact conversation and decision-making or it will be moved to the bottom of the priority list.

A typical outcome-focused agenda has three phases: (1) get grounded, (2) discuss and (3) land. "Get grounded" is your introduction—what you are going to accomplish, why it is important and how you are going to do it. "Discuss" is where you generate options, ideas and possibilities. Notice that "Discuss" is a talk verb. This is fine for one step in your agenda, just not as your end point. "Land" can represent a decision, plan, next steps—whatever your destination is.

Here's how Jeanine's meeting might look as a list of topics versus the three phases:

List of Topics Agenda	Structured Thought Pattern Agenda
Meeting Outcome: To review customer data and decide what we will act on and when	*Meeting Outcome: To review customer data and decide what we will act on and when*
9:00 – 9:15 Customer feedback on current pricing	9:00 – 9:15 Review key customer data on pricing and delivery method [Get grounded]
9:15 – 9:30 Customer feedback on new delivery method	9:15 – 9:45 Identify which issues have biggest impact on customer retention [Discuss]
9:30 – 10:00 Customer feedback on Returns policy	9:45 – 10:00 Determine next steps and owners for priority items [Land]

The agenda on the left is vague and only supports a "Talk" outcome. The agenda on the right supports Jeanine's outcome by providing steps that will guide the group's thinking from open-ended discussion to agreed-upon next steps. What's going to make this agenda really fly is Step 4: invite the right people and get them prepared.

Step 4. Invite the Right People and Get Them Prepared

I had a client who was becoming increasingly frustrated by the lack of progress in his meetings with a group of technical experts. They couldn't gain any traction; they couldn't reach decisions. The people in the meetings kept saying, "I'll have to get back to you." I asked him who these people went back to talk to and he identified two people—Francois and Hana. Clearly it was Francois and Hana who needed to be invited to the meetings, not these folks. Alternatively, Francois and Hana needed to deputize those attending with some decision-making authority.

Decision-makers or those they have deputized should be at the top of your invite list. Beyond these people, select wisely based on your outcome and agenda. Even in ongoing teams, there are no automatics on who to invite. Not every meeting needs to involve every person on your team. Decide who needs to be at the table and invite the appropriate people. Those without a defined purpose will distract, take up space and pull the meeting away from its intended outcome, leaving everyone feeling frustrated. This "agenda-based" participation should be transparent and, when possible, set up from the beginning of a project to prevent people from guessing or inventing why they weren't invited.

Invite lists are tricky in a cross-functional environment because so many people are involved. A friend of mine (and customer hub matrix player) told me a great story of a customer meeting. The list of attendees started to grow because everyone in the hub thought their attendance was critical. They showed up at the customer site, and the customer didn't have a conference room big enough, so half of them had to wait in the lobby.

As this story illustrates, there is great risk of overincluding in matrix roles. Strive to be inclusive but not all-inclusive. This is where having a clear outcome is critical, as is role clarity (Essential #3). Without these, narrowing the invite list becomes almost impossible. When you narrow, make sure you are transparent about it.

When considering your invite list, give it a litmus test. For each person, list why they must be there and what you expect them to do both in the meeting and as a result of the meeting. If there are a lot of "know," "understand" or "be aware of" statements, question whether they need to be there. These are the invite equivalents of talk verbs—"know verbs" that tell you a person needs to be informed, but not in attendance. There are a lot of ways to inform; meeting attendance is not required.

If you are being selective on whom to invite, make sure key people will be in attendance. If you call a meeting when you know key people can't come, you'll basically spend the meeting talking about what you wanted to talk about in the meeting—dancing around the topic, "Well, we'll have to wait to see what Jamel has to say before we can move forward on this." Decisions get deferred, more meetings are scheduled and you have to spend time bringing the absent people up to speed. Arrange the meeting for a time when you know key people can be there.

Once you get the invite list nailed down, think about how to make sure attendees are ready to hit the ground running at minute one of the meeting. Rarely do you want a group to walk in completely flat-footed, but you don't have to ask them to prepare 50 slides either. Give them something to do ahead of time, and don't just ask them to "think about" something. Ask them to bring something in—again think "physical," just like your outcome statement. Here are a few examples:

» Review and note which alternative…
» Identify three priorities…
» Bring in three concerns your team has…

This constitutes your prework and serves a specific purpose; it is not just a "nice to have." People don't do prework because they can slide by without it—they are busy, and this is one thing they can get away with not doing. Make it clear how you will use the prework and why it is imperative to do it. Let them know that you will be asking for this information in your cover note or in the prework itself, something like "I will ask each of you what you came in with…"

You can also build your prework into your agenda so they see how it is going to be used. Here's what Jeanine's agenda might look like with the prework embedded:

Meeting Outcome:
To review customer data and decide what we will act on and when

9:00 – 9:15: Review key customer data on pricing, delivery method
[PREWORK: **Please review attached Customer Visit Summary**]

9:15 – 9:45: Identify which issues have biggest impact on customer retention
[PREWORK: **Indicate your top three issues on the Customer Visit Summary**]

9:45 – 10:00: Determine next steps and owners for priority items
[PREWORK: **Identify people from your team who could play a role in resolution of your top three issues**]

She is giving them very specific instructions for their prework. It is not just something they need to review (and that they can easily skip). It is clear that they are actually going to talk about it—in other words be held accountable for the prework.

Don't be afraid to postpone a meeting if you walk in and find that people haven't done their homework. Set a precedent that when you include prework, it is required and adds value to the meeting. It isn't busy work. It usually only takes one cancellation to shift a group's behavior.

Lastly, give adequate notice whenever possible. Many people prefer to think things through ahead of time rather than speak off the cuff. Attendees who are highly organized will participate much more vigorously if they are given adequate time to prepare for the meeting. Show your discipline in planning and give user-friendly, realistic prework, and they will be fully engaged and ready to work, not wondering why they are there and what they are supposed to accomplish.

Step 5: Facilitate the Heck out of It

Have you ever participated in an elegantly facilitated meeting like Pete's meeting that I described in the introduction? It is a thing of beauty. People conflict but are heard and respected, and in the end they land on something. They walk away from the meeting feeling as if their time made a difference. Often such a meeting is the one thing they remember about the day as they drive home—there's a spot in my day that I accomplished something.

If you are wondering if you have ever facilitated such a meeting, I would ask you, have people ever gushed over one of your meetings? I find people make a point to tell you when it was a great, productive meeting. They spontaneously appreciate the fact that you gave everything you could so that their time was not wasted. They are grateful that yours was an island in a sea of crappy meetings.

So if people aren't gushing, you probably aren't facilitating, or at least not facilitating effectively. Another sign of good facilitation is exhaustion. If you don't walk away from facilitating a meeting feeling worn out, you probably aren't facilitating. When you facilitate, you do more than introduce the topics, watch the time and call the meeting to a close. You have to listen, connect all comments and stay several steps ahead to see where the conversation is going and determine whether you will need to redirect. Your mind never wanders: you are 100% attentive, 100% of the time. I have a life goal of being present. It is so hard for me. But put me in a room with a team of people and a tough decision and my mind never wanders; there is too much at risk.

It isn't easy, but people appreciate good facilitation so much because they feel like you just took their time and ideas and helped them mold it into something meaningful. A good facilitator can make even modest progress seem huge.

Facilitation is a skill that matrix managers use in almost every conversation they have. If you are the traffic cop or connector between two sides of the matrix, you are constantly bringing people and ideas together. Meetings just happen to be the formal, public version of this.

FACILITATOR ROLES

Facilitation is a complex skill best learned by watching others. Don't have any skilled facilitators around? The good news is you can learn from nonexamples as well. And there are plenty of poor facilitators out there!

Here are the key roles that a facilitator plays. Every group and every topic will require a different combination and proportion of these roles.

- » Keep focus
- » Connect ideas
- » Balance participation
- » Keep things moving toward desired outcome
- » Manage time

KEEP FOCUS

I remember a small group of senior folks that I was attempting to facilitate early in my career. For many different reasons, their meetings were a train wreck. At one point, I literally stood on a chair waving my hands in an attempt to get them back on track. Keeping focus is arguably the most challenging of facilitator roles. Tangents, side conversations and personal conflicts lurk around every corner. The good news is that there is more at your disposal than standing on a chair like a mad woman.

First and foremost, you need to keep the meeting's outcome at the forefront. You can do this by posting your outcome somewhere everyone can see like the wall or top of the agenda. Introduce each part of the meeting by stating the goal for that issue and describing the process you plan to use. This helps everyone focus on the same task.

Keep the conversation focused by referring back to the objective and agenda.

ZOOM OUT

You can also keep things on track by referring to the agenda, *"That's a great point, we will get to that a little later in the agenda—write it down and remind me if I don't bring it up when we get there."* Or, if it doesn't fall within the parameters of your agenda, use a "parking lot" to capture important topics that should be discussed at another time. If you commit to discussing a topic later in the meeting or put it in a parking lot, be sure you actually go back to it. If the topic is outside the meeting's scope, say so. Don't create the illusion that it is something to be addressed.

Finally, you will need to keep the individual energy and attention focused on the task, not extracurricular interpersonal issues. Conflicts come up in group settings, and whether it is a personal attack on you or someone else, as the facilitator you need to respond to it.

Your first response to a disruptive comment or behavior should be subtle. Reframe the comment in a positive way. If Kiara, a participant in Jeanine's customer data meeting, gets fired up and says, "Roger, it's no wonder the customer reacted that way. You and your team have been completely negligent on this for months," attempt to restate her criticism, minus the emotion: "OK, Kiara, you think the customer reaction can be tracked back to some negligence on our part.

Where do you think we are falling short?" Take the finger-pointing out of it and don't match the tone. If you are Kiara's target, pause for a minute. You will be surprised how many times the group jumps in for you. Don't rush to defend. As a facilitator, you don't want to be seen as leveraging the position to defend yourself. If you pause and no one jumps in, reframe it much the way you would if it were directed toward someone else.

If the subtle approach doesn't work, be more direct. Don't match their tone, but address the tone. So, if Kiara doesn't respond to the subtle approach and keeps attacking Roger or you, say something like, "Kiara, this is the second time you've brought this up today, and it is obvious you are pretty frustrated. If this is something you need to talk to Roger about offline, then that is great, but right now we need to channel some of that energy toward the solution." You can use the same approach if you are in the crosshairs: acknowledge the emotion, suggest talking about it outside the meeting and ask to channel comments toward the solution.

When you have to address a negative behavior, remember that while the offender may be a bit chastised, everyone else in the meeting will inwardly be applauding you. Also keep in mind that often your role as facilitator gives your comments extra weight. You probably will not need to come down too hard—just acknowledging the behavior is more than is usually done, and usually enough to get someone to back off. You also need to tread lightly because chances are if this person is in a meeting with you they are an ongoing part of your matrix, and the relationship needs to be preserved.

> When responding to a disruptive comment, stay neutral. Restate the information, minus the tone.
>
> **JUJITSU**

CONNECT IDEAS

A facilitator colleague of mine calls this "stopping the plopping." Left to their own devices, groups can throw out comments, ideas and opinions randomly, without connecting or building on each other's thoughts. When they start to "plop," what you get in the end is a "pile of plop" (her words, not mine) in the middle of the table, but no synthesized pool of thought. It's OK for rapid-fire brainstorming, but as an ongoing meeting practice, it is not constructive.

When you connect ideas, you are comparing or combining comments. Doing this helps manage and mold the pile on the table. It shows progress toward the goal, highlights common ground and gradually builds toward a shared idea. Here are some examples of statements that manage the plop:

*"That's sounds similar to what Julietta said [specific comment]—
is that fair to say?"*

*"So compare that to what Wayne mentioned earlier about [spe-
cific comment]—is this an example of what he had proposed?*

*"I've heard several people mention issues around [specific
topic]—do we have some agreement that this might be an area
of focus?"*

Notice that all of these connections are tentative, and you are asking for verification. Verifying the connection makes sure that you have heard correctly, and it shows people that you expect them to listen and build on each other's ideas. Often after a few prompts from you, they will start their own connecting.

State your connections tentatively; ask for verification.

JUJITSU

BALANCE PARTICIPATION

Getting talkative people to pull back or quiet people to speak up is a challenge. Some people talk to be heard or think out loud and end up repeating themselves or others. Others only speak up if they are committed to what they are going to say. You invited people to the meeting to hear all perspectives, not just a handful, so you need to work to balance the participation.

Here are a few ways to help your more outgoing participants take a step back and let others into the conversation:

*"Ok, so tell me how your comment compares to Paula's—are you
agreeing with what Paula said or is there a difference in there
we should hear?"*

(Makes it clear that there is no need to repeat what others are
saying just to have something to say and makes it clear that
you'd better listen to what others are saying—not just throw
stuff out).

"OK, let's hear from a few others."

*"We heard from Cora and Carlos; what are some other perspec-
tives that don't fall into these two points of view?"*

To get the quieter folks to speak up, try throwing out a question and then going around the table. Nonverbally encourage them to speak up by leaning forward, making eye contact and nodding. Look for subtle signs that they have something to say—a quick hand up, vigorous nodding or prolonged eye contact with you may all be signs they are ready to speak up.

Sometimes it is not personal preference that holds people back, it's the topic. When a topic becomes dominated by just two or three people and the rest are shutting off, it may be that the topic or the level of detail is not applicable to everyone. Encourage the interested parties to take it offline: "It sounds like those are some pretty specific tactics for the two of you to work out—why don't you take that offline, and we will pull things back to the bigger picture for this meeting."

KEEP THINGS MOVING

The best way to keep things moving toward your outcome is to continually tell people where you are vis-à-vis your outcome. Progress breeds progress, which in turn leads to satisfaction with the meeting and the overall process/project. It keeps people engaged and hopeful. After completing a major part of the meeting, summarize what the group accomplished. This is one of the reasons that Pete's meetings were so motivating. When he summarized, he was celebrating the achievement, reminding everyone what they finished and formally ending the discussion.

Keep the energy of the group alive by stepping back to see progress toward the goal. **ZOOM OUT**

Show bigger-picture progress too, by beginning your meetings with what was accomplished since the last meeting. "Last time we talked about x, and here's how it has been implemented." If you don't want people to feel like meetings are pointless, you have to offer some proof that they're not.

Synthesizing ideas and comments shows progress too. After a period of time generating ideas, synthesize what you have heard: "So it sounds like our options fall into four categories [list them out, ideally on a flipchart or screen]. Am I missing any?" This tightens up the discussion and moves things toward the next phase.

You will also have to help the group move forward when they become stuck. When this happens, start by labeling it and then summarize where you are and where you need to go: "It sounds like we are a little stuck. So far I have heard us identify three possible solutions, but we need to land on one to proceed with…" If that nudge doesn't move them, try to help them figure out what might get them unstuck. It may be more information, bringing another person into the discussion or just walking away for a bit. Don't let the wheels spin. Help them stay in the conversation by figuring out a way to get unstuck.

MANAGING TIME

A facilitator, while not a timekeeper (if you need one of those, delegate the task), needs to help the group be mindful of time. A good agenda helps here. Reminders and time checks like these help keep things moving: "You'll see on the agenda we have just 15 minutes to discuss this, so we will need to stay focused and on topic." "We've got about 5 minutes left on this part of the agenda, let's take one last thought and then wrap things up."

You will also need to help manage time when the group has taken a detour and that detour is impacting the timing of the meeting. If it is a positive detour, renegotiate the time parameters: "We are set to spend just five more minutes on this—but it seems like we are covering good ground—everyone OK if we either stay on an extra five minutes or take five minutes from the next agenda item?" When the detour does not appear to add value, note it and ask them to move on. What you must do is avoid unconscious departure from the agenda: you don't want to wander.

Time management starts with beginning the meeting on time. Don't recap for late people. Doing so legitimizes lateness and disrespects those who made an effort to show up on time. Also make sure you end on time. If you must run over, check in with the group. Repeatedly running over should tell you something—your agenda is too ambitious or your facilitation needs to be tighter. Finally, never be afraid to end a meeting early. A meeting that accomplishes its objective in less than the allotted time is a victory, and you are the hero.

The tone for all of these facilitator roles is pragmatic and no-nonsense. Not school marm—you are not there to shame into compliance. Setting up ground rules at the beginning of the meeting can help here. Ground rules set expectations and can serve as a starting point for correcting behavior. "We agreed to make sure that everyone was heard today, and I don't think we have heard Colleen's opinion on this yet." Ground rules can be set around level of participation, use of technology/multitasking, confidentiality or problem (versus personal) focus.

A bit of self-deprecating humor also helps diffuse many situations and can help maintain relationships and participation of the group, "OK, I will play the bad cop here and say that we are breaking a few ground rules." "I don't know about you, but I feel like we have gotten lost—let me attempt to find us again."

Finally, your role as facilitator does not include filling the silence with comments. Allow silence, it gives people time to think and absorb. If you need to, check in on the silence: "So, help me read the silence—are we lost or just thinking?"

For really sticky situations a professional may be needed. But don't become overreliant on third parties to lead your meetings. For teams that are longer-term, facilitation should be a group skill, one that everyone gets good at. A great way to do this is through training, but also consider having a professional facilitator come in for a short period of time to demonstrate the right behavior and build good habits in the team, then send them off to facilitate on their own.

Step 6. Follow Up and Hold Accountable

Your responsibilities as the meeting facilitator don't end with the close of the meeting. Following up on commitments and holding participants accountable sets the next meeting up for success—they make your meeting serious business. Often we fail to manage this "white space" and rely entirely on meetings to stand on their own. In established teams with a strong sense of accountability and a consistent meeting process, the meetings may not need follow-up. For all others, follow-up is required.

Follow-up starts with having good notes on the meeting. I hesitate to call them "minutes" because this label connotes verbatim transcription. Notes should really be a summary of who was there, what was decided, what the next steps are and who owns those next steps. Make them easy to read, with "Decisions Made" clearly marked, as well as "Next Steps." Then share them with participants and key stakeholders. "I shared our follow-ups with [a common boss, project sponsor], and she thinks they make a ton of sense."

But depending on the length of time between meetings and the maturity of your meeting process, the documentation might not be enough. If this is the case, follow-up to the group or specific individuals will ensure that your next meeting is structured appropriately (based on actual progress) and doesn't start right back from square one. This "white space" management keeps the momentum going and provides continuity for your next meeting. As mentioned in Essential #4, without follow-up the space between meetings is where decisions die. The same is true of ideas and to-do's: they can easily fade to black in the white space.

When You Aren't Leading the Meeting

Realistically, there will be plenty of meetings in your matrix that you participate in, versus lead. When you aren't leading the meeting or the project, trying to get others to adopt the principles in this chapter can be tricky. Here are a few subtle ways to shift other people's meeting behavior:

Guilt. Be the best meeting attendee ever. Ask questions, connect what people are saying, redirect conversation. Be on time. Be disciplined. Guilt everyone else into behaving better.

Volunteer. Ask the meeting leader if they want your help in agenda planning. They may view this as a welcome relief.

Demonstrate. Informally facilitate during the meeting—ask opinions, link, contrast and compare comments.

Coax. Ask questions to push a meeting leader to be more deliberate in thinking through the meeting: "What results do you think we want from the meeting? I'd like to show up prepared." "How will we choose which plan to use? I'd like to think through options ahead of time." These are questions the leader should be considering, and knowing you are one step ahead of them may push them to think things through.

Be direct. The direct approach can also be used—just frame it in a way that is all about making everyone's lives easier and advancing the project: "I noticed that we tend to spin our wheels in the first part of our meetings. I am wondering if an agenda and some prework might help us hit the ground running and get us to resolutions faster."

All the talk in these matrix roles is not cheap, but we treat it like it is. Rarely do we treat meetings with the reverence they deserve—you are bringing together (live or virtually) your matrix. This is it—a test for you as a matrix master and an opportunity to do what the matrix is intended to do—bring together multiple parts of the business to solve problems that can't be solved in a vacuum.

Invest by deliberately planning and tactfully facilitating your meetings. They won't all be perfect—they may even get worse before they get better as you try out some of these approaches. Learn from these bad experiences, as well as the meetings that people say positive things about. If someone says it was a great meeting, ask him or her what made it good.

G ood meeting facilitation is not common practice. Few people have the skills, and most of us sit through poorly run meetings, develop a lot of bad habits and then, when it's our turn to step up and lead, just don't have the skills to do it. Become an observer. Some of the best facilitation techniques are very, very subtle. Notice what effective facilitators say and do to move a group forward. Take these approaches and blend them with your own style of expressing things for really powerful facilitation that you will use daily in your matrix role—in meetings and out.

IN SUMMARY

EMBRACE

→ Meetings matter. They are not a departure from work; in a matrix they are your work, and you get out of them what you put into them.

→ A structured, discipline approach to planning them, which starts with a clear outcome.

→ Your role as an active facilitator. There is not a role you can play that will be as appreciated as much as this is. People are grateful for those who don't waste their time and help them create something they couldn't on their own.

→ Your role in managing the "white space" between meetings—don't let the matrix drown out all the work that was done and assigned in your meeting. Follow up and keep it alive.

→ Your role as a meeting participant. Even if you aren't leading the meeting, there are safe, subtle ways to make it better.

WHERE TO START

→ Give your meeting outcome the "on the table" test. Ask yourself what you want to be sitting in the middle of the table at the end of the meeting. This will help you structure your agenda and facilitate effectively.

→ Check your agenda; make sure it reflects a thought process, not a list of topics

→ Keep the purpose of the meeting visible—it helps keep conversation on track and can keep people motivated toward the accomplishment

→ As the leader, keep track of the follow-up nudges you will need to provide in the white space so that decisions and tasks don't get lost between meetings

IN PRACTICE

FOR LEADERS

I don't care how high up in the organization you are, you have to be good at this. Even if you are so high up that others do the heavy lifting on meetings, you need to appreciate what it looks like when it is done well. You set the expectation on how they are run and how well used the time is. Never believe this is "beneath you." Also, never let team meetings take the place of one-to-ones. This is common practice. Leaders get busy, and they pull everyone in to get informed. That is a really expensive way to get informed, and the outcome is really frustrated, stressed (because they just lost time) team members. Be disciplined about one-to-ones and use team meetings strategically and with purpose.

FOR CROSS-FUNCTIONAL/MATRIX TEAMS

Meetings are your most important collective competency as a cross-functional team, and they often indicate the overall function/dysfunction of the team. Adopt a handful of practices that you all adhere to and hold each other accountable for. Check in on the effectiveness of meetings at least every 6 months—what is working, what is not, what needs to change. If you get good at this, you will pick up speed, make better decisions and gain credibility. This is your vehicle—be mindful of this competency and continually hone it.

WORKING VIRTUALLY

The good practices for in-person meetings become nonnegotiables in virtual meetings. The discipline, structure and deliberate effort described in this chapter are absolutely essential. I believe that with virtual, every interaction should be treated as a formal meeting—that means everything has some structure and guidelines, no loose wandering online conversations. And, we have to find ways to replicate the "before the meeting starts" dialogue that is so critical. Don't forget this—it can come in the form of a silly opening question or round robin on how everyone's weekend was, or simply individual notes in chat to check in. We can get pretty task-focused with online meetings, so you will have to work to build in the personal time. Even simple connections in a meeting can help build trust and camaraderie. Last, as you can tell from the suggestions, video on. Always. Most people I talk to now say there are really no conference calls anymore, they are all video. This is good. It doesn't replace in-person, but it is much, much easier to get things done when you see faces.

BONUS MATERIAL: WHAT TO HIRE FOR

This book and learning sessions alone can't ensure success in working cross-functionally. We have to start further back in the employee life cycle. We need to stack our deck through hiring for these abilities.

Obviously, I recommend interviewing with the 7 Essentials in mind. Below are potential interview questions and what to look for in the candidate's answers. Cross-functional work is intuitive for some, but not all, and you need to understand who you have in front of you.

Master the Matrix Essential	Questions	What to Look For
Partnerships	How would you describe the role that partnerships/relationships play in your ability to get things done? How would you go about building partnerships in a new role? Describe a time when you had to rebuild or repair a partnership. What steps did you take?	Understanding of the importance of relationships and trust, initiative in identifying and cultivating partnerships, taking responsibility when partnerships need repair
Goals	Describe a time when you had conflicting priorities. How did you tackle this?	Appreciation of big-picture goals (beyond their own priorities), willingness to give and take with others, initiative in resolving these conflicts
Roles	Describe a time when your role (in general or on a project or task) was ambiguous. How did you navigate this?	Comfort in figuring things out (versus expecting things to be laid out in black and white); initiative to resolve, problem-solving mindset versus territorialism
Decision-Making	Give me an example of a decision where you had to bring others in (or one where you should have brought others in and didn't).	Casting a wide net for stakeholders, using a structured approach to bring them in and get the decision made, insights and quick recovery if it was less than successful
Influence	What and who do you influence in your current role? How do you approach it?	Ability to articulate specific tactics, orientation, etc.—sees the idea or recommendation outside of their own perspective
Communication	How do you make sure your key partnerships (teammates, bosses) are well informed?	Deliberate steps to understand the information needs of others, a process for checking in, readily admits "misses" in communication
Meetings	When you are planning a meeting, how do you approach it?	Mindset—do they see the meeting as potential to make progress or do they approach reluctantly, and what do they do to prepare (specifically, do they consider a concrete, clear objective as an important step in the process?)

PUTTING IT ALL TOGETHER

So You Have Finished the Book, Now What?

Here are a few things to consider:

IT STARTS WITH YOU. Just like the principle we talked about in Essential #1, it starts with you, and you should keep on doing it even when no one else is following suit. Don't wait for the organization to improve its matrix, improve your own.

DON'T RELY ON ONE ESSENTIAL FOR YOUR SUCCESS; you will need more than that for sustained achievement. Make it your goal to improve in other areas, don't just continue to leverage one strength.

THE 7 ESSENTIALS WORK IN CONCERT. Don't try to find one panacea. If you or your team is struggling, look at multiple diagnoses and solutions.

CHANGE THE CONVERSATION. Too much of our talk about cross-functional work revolves around complaints and criticism. This book provides a framework and language for discussing the matrix constructively. Whether it is discussing human-made versus natural goal misalignments or role clarity versus role acceptance, this book can serve as a foundation for diagnosing issues in an objective way.

KEEP LEARNING. Here are a few of the resources I mentioned in the book (and a few others that I turn to often) that will help you in your journey:

Crucial Conversations and Crucial Confrontations
Patterson et al. 2002, 2005

Decision Traps: The Ten Barriers to Brilliant Decision-Making and How to Overcome Them
Russo and Schoemaker, 1989

Getting Together: Building Relationships as We Negotiate
Fisher and Brown, 1988

The Trusted Advisor
Maister et al. 2000

How to Decide: Simple Tools for Making Better Choices
Anne Duke, 2020

Leading Organization Design: How to Make Organization Design Decisions to Drive the Results You Want
Kesler and Kates, 2010

Networked, Scaled, and Agile: A Design Strategy for Complex Organizations
Kates, Kesler, et al., 2021

Predictably Irrational
Dan Ariely, 2010

Think Again: The Power of Knowing What You Don't Know
Adam Grant, 2021

The 7 Habits of Highly Effective People Anniversary Edition
Stephen R. Covey, Sean Covey, 2020

The Triangle of Truth: The Surprisingly Simple Secret to Resolving Conflicts Large and Small
Lisa Earle McLeod, 2010

 FINERTYCONSULTING.COM

The Finerty Consulting website is designed to meet the demands of complex organizations. It's specifically organized to be a mobile tool for Matrix Mastery and Cross-Functional Influence development. From daily tips to monthly featured videos, there's a wealth of materials and resources including In-Person, Digital and On-Demand Learning.

180°ASSESSMENT

Are you close to Matrix Mastery? What do your cross-functional stakeholders think of your influence approach? Find out with our multisource assessment tools that provide feedback on individual effectiveness as well as what is most critical for your role. Find out with Matrix 180, the multisource feedback instrument that provides feedback on individual effectiveness in the 7 requirements of matrix mastery!

e-LEARNING

The Master the Matrix e-Learning course is a great way to encourage ongoing dialogue and learning, especially for geographically dispersed organizations. Finerty Consulting provides e-Learning modules that are interactive, practical and application-based. Go to finertyconsulting.talentmls.com.

WORKSHOPS

Our virtual and in-person workshops are perfect for anyone in a matrix role! For groups of ten or more.

KEEP IN TOUCH!

Connect with other matrix practitioners at
www.finertyconsulting.com!

Contact us at info@finertyconsulting.com

ACKNOWLEDGMENTS

Six months after the first edition of this book came out, I called Kevin Fitzgerald (who beautifully designed this book, does all my graphic design and was in the middle of redesigning my website) and said, "Take everything off the website except the matrix stuff, it's all I want to do." I believe his reply was something like, "Ah, you sure? That seems like a pretty big decision, and it's 9 o'clock at night. Maybe you should sleep on it?"

I didn't look back. Anything nonmatrix was handed to other consultants, —I wanted to take this bit of content and do everything with it—teach, consult, assess, coach—everything.

It has been an amazing 10 years, and it changed my voice. Those of you who read the first edition probably noticed. I feel much more definitive with this one. *Master the Matrix* was the first book to look at matrix organizations from a practitioner's point of view. It was my first book, and based only on my own experience and my research. I went a lot off gut, validated by some research, but a lot on gut, and took a leap and said, "This is how you should do it."

And it worked. Tens of thousands of books and thousands of workshop participants, consulting and coaching clients later, I'm definitive. My voice is confident. I have seen a lot—I have felt your frustrations, seen your successes, heard your questions and been warmed by your praise. Working cross-functionally will never be easy, but this model helps people make sense of it and get traction.

What hasn't changed is the cast of characters that made this possible. Once again, Emilie Croisier, my editor, is such a trusted partner and amazing soul. As mentioned, Kevin Fitzgerald is a wizard of book design. I think sometimes these two know what I am trying to say before I do! Julia Curtis was my intern and data cruncher—if, at this writing, that girl isn't employed, somebody needs to grab her. Wise beyond her years and a work ethic like I have never seen before.

My kids are no longer little and living at home and wondering why Mommy is holed up in her office. I think (hope) they can now see this book for what it is—my life's passion. And when you have a passion and your gut tells you "go"— you go. Meg, Abby and Sean—please promise me to always, always follow your passion.

Over 1,500 people participated in some way in the research for this edition—

through surveys or assessments or interviews. Here are a few that went above and beyond to help:

Helen Brausen	Aditi Gokhale	Don Robertson
Beth Dawson	Clay Isbell	A. G. Rudd
Nancy Evans	Art Mollenhauer	Shabnoor Shah
Tim Finnegan	Cheryl Pape	Deb Skarda
Bill Fleming	Raj Patel	Mike Warenski
Daniel George	Mike Rittenhouse	

And a special thanks to Tony Thelen, my foreword author and early adopter of all things "matrix." People always ask me, "What companies work really well cross-functionally?" My answer is always, "I don't know a singular company that does it well in every part of the organization, but I know of pockets." And then I tell them about Tony.

Go forth and master it.

ABOUT THE AUTHOR

Susan Finerty is the author of *Master the Matrix: 7 Essentials for Getting Things Done in Complex Organizations, Cross-Functional Influence: Getting Things Done Across the Organization* and *Cross-Functional Influence Playbook*. In 2004, she established a consulting practice focused on organizational effectiveness—helping organizations design and implement change, helping teams work effectively together and coaching individuals. Prior to founding her consultancy, she worked in organization development positions at Baxter Healthcare and two small pharmaceutical companies.

She now focuses exclusively on helping matrix organizations and matrix practitioners get results through working cross-functionally.

Susan Zelmanski Finerty

Susan has held adjunct faculty roles at Northwestern University and currently teaches at University of Wisconsin-Madison School of Business. She has a BA from Central Michigan University and an MA from Indiana University. Susan resides in suburban Chicago and can usually be found paddleboarding, gardening, chasing her dogs or bragging about her three kids.

Made in United States
Troutdale, OR
09/26/2023

13200112R00110